THE FISHERMAN'S YEARBOOK 19..
COARSE · GAME · SEA

edited by Nigel Flynn

ISBN 0 7117 0350 7

Designed and produced by PARKE SUTTON Limited,
8 Thorpe Road, Norwich NR1 1RY for
Jarrold Colour Publications, Barrack Street, Norwich NR3 1TR

Text copyright © 1988 Nigel Flynn
The edition copyright © 1988 Jarrold Colour Publications

All rights reserved. No part of this publication may be reproduced,
stored in a retrieval system or transmitted, in any form or by any means,
electronic, mechanical, photocopying, recording or otherwise, without the
prior permission of the publisher.

Whilst every effort has been made to ensure that the information given
in this book is correct at the time of going to press, no responsibility
can be accepted by the publishers or Parke Sutton Limited for any errors
or inaccuracies that may appear.

Printed in England.

CONTENTS

John Bailey's Coarse Fishing Year 05
Pike Fishing by Ken Whitehead 18
Country Code for Anglers 24
Active Carp Fishing by Chris Yates 25
The Water Authorities of England and Wales 28
South West Water Open Seasons 33
Welsh Water Open Seasons 36
The Administration of Fisheries in Scotland and Northern Ireland 37
The Game Fishing Year by Trevor Housby 40
Trevor Housby's Guide to Reservoir Trout Fishing in England and Wales 45
National Bodies, Clubs and Associations 49
Law and the Angler by Michael Gregory, L.L.B. 56
The Freshwater and Saltwater Fishes of the British Isles by Len Cacutt 58
New Tackle by John Wilson 81
John Wilson's Guide to UK Tackle Dealers 90
The Sea Angling Year by Mike Millman 95
Safety Afloat and Ashore 106
Do's and Don'ts at Sea 108
Weather Forecasts 109
The Beaufort Wind Scale 110
Tide Tables 112
Fishing Diary for 1989 117
The Contributors 144

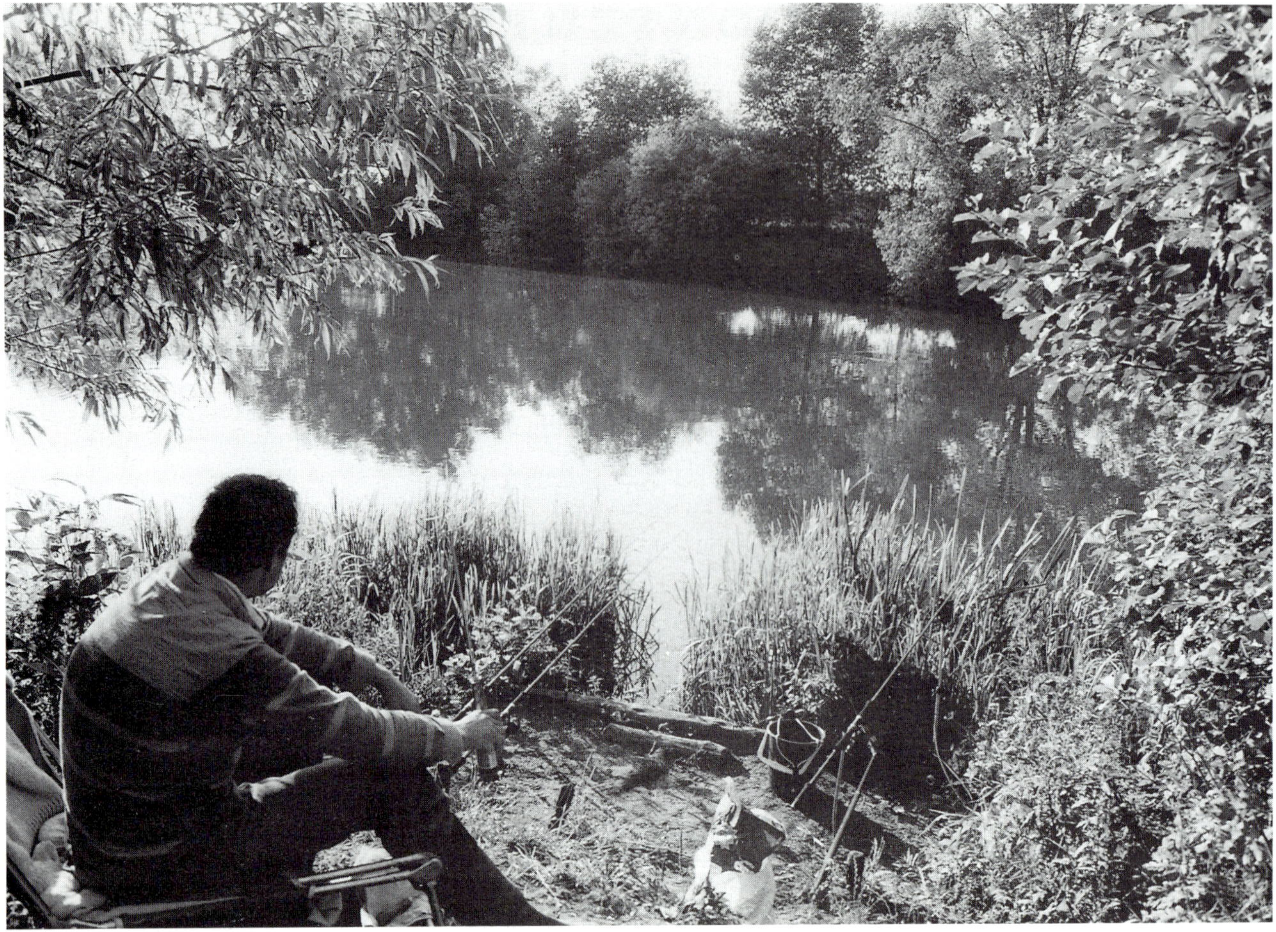

JOHN BAILEY'S
COARSE FISHING YEAR

'There is nothing, absolutely nothing,' writes Norfolk angler John Bailey, 'better than being a coarse fisherman. Every month of the year there is a different aspect of the sport waiting for you to taste and enjoy. This is a shame for those specialists who pursue a single species of fish: they miss the most amazing challenges and variety.' Guided by a fishing strategy he has followed for fifteen years, John Bailey takes us through the coarse fisherman's year in all its richness. 'Follow this plan,' says the author, 'and I promise you will not regret it. Fish well and by the close of the year you will have had some superb fish and marvellous memories to sustain you forever.'

Spring, summer, autumn and winter all bring differing conditions for the angler, and an immense variety of species to pursue.

January

The start of the new year can be a nightmare of wild weather: floods, frosts, gales and snows that rip the weeks apart and destroy water conditions for nearly every species but the chub. This bold, biting river fish is a true angler's friend, for there is never a day in winter when one, somewhere in the river, will not have a go at a well-presented bait.

January river fishing for chub, however, is not always easy. Sometimes it is necessary to walk miles casting into every likely hole under trees or into deeper slacks. It never pays to sit too long over fish unwilling to feed, and to keep on the move greatly increases the chances of success.

Baits need to be carefully selected. If the water has colour to it, a pungent piece of luncheon meat or cheese will score over maggot or breadflake. Sometimes cold water chub will only look at a tiny piece on a small hook, but, on occasion, a great chunk on a size 4 will be engulfed – perhaps representing the fish's only meal of the day.

Bites vary enormously. A mere shiver on the rod tip, as though the wind has plucked it, is typical. Then, out of the snow-laden sky, could come a pull that takes the rod off the rests. Such is the charm of chub; you never know what will happen next. But what is certain is that the fish of January will be in the finest condition: beautifully bronzed and fat as butter. They will also fight ferociously in the cold rush of the winter river.

Tip for the month

For shy chub try a piece of sprat on a size 6 hook. It is an unusual bait and gives off a strong scent in cloudy water. You will find that some chub will love it.

February

Notoriously, February is a month of high pressure, clear, frosty nights and bitter days made worse by easterly winds. Very often all still waters are frozen, so the fisherman must return to the rivers for the chub's smaller cousin, the dace. This small, silver fish seems immune to the cold. I have caught them when the daytime temperature has been 26.6 °F (−3 °C) and when ice has formed on the rod rings as I reeled in.

In the gin-clear rivers of a typical February, the very lightest tackle is essential. This is the time to trot the water with a stick float, size 18 or 20 hook and single maggot, caster or tiny

Chub in January are not always easy to find or catch.

red worm. The hook-length should never be more than 2 lb (1 kg) breaking strain and often must be less. Look for the runs of steady pace, between 3–6 ft (1–1.8 m) deep, over a gravel bed if possible, and there you will find dace. Explore all the twists and turns of the current with your float and feed in maggots sparingly. Soon fish will come your way.

They will not be big, for a half-pound (227g) fish is a good one, but they will fight hard on gossamer tackle and look like slivers of silver in the afternoon sunlight. You will probably be the only man out on such a day. Enjoy the solitude, return your fish and crunch home early as the frost begins to crackle on the banks at sunset.

Tip for the month
For the largest dace, try fishing at dusk and during the first hour of darkness. Use breadflake on a size 12 hook and ledger it in a deeper area of moderately paced water. Put a slice or two of mashed bread in as an attractant and watch for bites on a quivertip illuminated by a torch-beam.

March

Frosts are no longer so severe, the afternoon sun has some strength to it and, in the early evening, there are fly hatches over the water. Waterfowl are pairing up and spring is on its way: it is the time for big roach.

A fine haul of roach.

Just before the end of the coarse fishing season, roach are at their very best. In the peak of condition, they are fine-looking fish, with deep flanks and deep colouring. This is the time the shoals group before spawning. Find one of these traditional spawning areas and a bonanza of fishing is all but guaranteed. The lengths upriver of mills are always worth investigating. So too are deep areas of steady flow over a clean bottom where a few water cabbages grow.

Slow trotting is the key method now. The bait, either flake or double maggot, should be fished slightly overdepth and the float held back to move down somewhat slower than the current itself. When roach bite on this rig, it is with a slow determination which makes them almost unmissable. A good roach might not fight with breathtaking speed or power, but there is majesty in its head-shaking anger. Land a 2 lb (1 kg) roach and you will not find a more impressive fish anywhere in Britain today: it is no wonder that for centuries it has been the coarseman's favourite fish. Taken now, it makes the arrival of the closed season just bearable.

Tip for the month
It always pays to be on the roach river at dawn. At that time, individual fish frequently head and shoulder in a slow roll, giving away the location of the shoal. Remember too that rolling fish are feeding fish.

APRIL/MAY

Historically, these are the months when the coarse fisherman gardens, decorates and goes through his tackle – in other words, kicks his heels and nearly dies of boredom! But this enforced idleness is only unavoidable for a few anglers. Some take to fly fishing while others sea fish off some nearby coast. The wisest will use the time to fish for eels.

Water Authorities have differing rules for closed season eeling and it is necessary to check the bye-laws regarding hook sizes and bait before commencing.

Many river catchment areas hold a good head of eels, hidden in ponds and lakes which are fed by the streams followed by elvers as babies from the sea. There the elvers stay to grow to a large size before maturing and departing for the sea by way of the feeder stream and parent river to the coast. Later, the eels gather in the Sargasso area of the Atlantic Ocean. After mating, the adults die and the resulting elvers begin the cycle of life once again.

A warm May evening by a lake (having first obtained permission to fish) is the best time and place to start eeling. For bait use some kind of dead fish, secure on a big hook and 10 lb or 12 lb (4.5 – 5.4 kg) line. The rod, too, should not be less than 2 lb (1 kg) test curve, as a big eel can really pull.

Put the baits out near any underwater focal point such as an island or a fallen tree, click back the reel bail arms and wait until the sun has descended and darkness falls. When an eel runs, the line will hiss off the reel and away into the lake. Strike quickly – you do not want a deep-hooked fish that will die – and prepare to pump and pump until your arms ache and the eel is finally yours.

Do not worry too much about unhooking a large eel, for they lie fairly quiet on wet sacking. A twist of the forceps will free the hook from the lip. Let the eel go and watch it wriggle into the gloom to fulfil its part in nature's plan.

Tip for the month
The important thing about eel baits is that they must be fresh. Small, fresh, coarse fish are best, followed by smelt or sardine.

JUNE

No fish is more beloved than the June tench. Generations of coarse anglers have considered no other species with which to start the new season on the glorious sixteenth. The tench has nearly always repaid this faith, for it is a generous fish – bold biting at times, always hard fighting and spectacular to hold and look at. The smooth olive skin, paddle-shaped fins and pin-prick red eyes make it distinctive among British freshwater fish.

Bait the swim a week or so before the new season. Almost any bait will do and a mixture of sweetcorn, bread, maggots and worms is as good a base as any. Choose a swim close to rushes – bullrushes are best of all – and one that has a hard or clean sand bottom. Too much silt or foul mud and the tench will simply not feed there.

Be at the swim before dawn on the sixteenth. Watch the mist rise and the new season's sun lighten the sky and glow over your swim. With luck the tench will be moving, creating patches of bubbles and displacing sediment which will drift to the surface. The best rig is undoubtedly a small wind-beater float, shotted right down with the bait just brushing the bottom.

Strike the instant the tip disappears, for tench give anglers less and less time as waters become more heavily fished.

Tranquil scenes fishing for tench (above) and Bream (opposite).

However appealing the bait, tench are ready to bolt at the slightest suspicion.

Looking back at the hundreds of tench landed in my career, I can recall the fight of nearly every one in detail. From striking to netting, the battle is fierce from this pluckiest of all fish. No tench is ever forgotten and to land a four-pounder (1.8 kg) is worth all the hard work and lack of sleep. There is no better start to the season.

Tip for the month
Tench adore the taste and smell of boiled hempseed. Mix a quarter of a pint (0.141 l) in with your groundbait and the small black seeds will keep the tench in your swim for hours.

JULY

July is the month I go night fishing on the pits and lakes of Norfolk. Night-time is spellbinding in the summer countryside. Fishing becomes a magical experience and the angler is never more at one with nature. I love the dark hours then – the time for the biggest of still water bream.

Bream are not the most fashionable species at present, but that will change as more anglers realise the challenge they present. Big bream are old, careful fish and to land one over 7 lb or 8 lb (3 – 3.6 kg) is some achievement. They might not fish hard but they become very wary and hook-shy, and such fish are difficult to overcome.

I tend to choose one water and stay on it, whether pit or lake, until the bream are mastered. I choose a quiet swim facing the prevailing wind and prepare it with bait day after day. Results will improve as time goes by and more and more bream become conditioned to the fact that a steady supply of food awaits them.

Top up the swim with bait an hour before dusk. I almost always use particles – grains of white rice, sweetcorn, casters, even some sultanas. Mixed in a fine groundbait, I catapult them the required distance or, for preference, take the baits out by boat and drop them with pinpoint accuracy in the swim.

I nearly always ledger at night with fine lines of 3 lb or 4 lb (1.3 – 1.8 kg) breaking strain. The end tackle is a fixed paternoster with a 4 ft or 5ft (1 – 1.5 m) hook length to give the bream plenty of time to mouth the bait before feeling any resistance. The peaks of action are usually the two hours after dark and the hour before dawn. If, however, the weather is grey and the water choppy, bream may feed until mid-morning.

Tip for the month
This might sound foolish, but the reedy margins of lakes are havens for midges in high summer and, in the evening and warm night-time, they bite least. Never go without an adequate supply of insect repellent. I have found *Jungle Formula* to be the most effective.

August

As the harvest begins there is nothing more appealing than to hunt rudd on the surface of local lakes, pools and pits. After tench and perch, rudd are the third most lovely-looking British freshwater fish and to take them 'off the top' on fly or floating crust is a real thrill.

I generally begin in the late afternoon when the water is milky warm and the rudd shoals are well in the upper layers, generally basking under overhanging willow or alder. Well-soaked *Chum* dog biscuit is my favourite bait and, when catapulted towards the trees, it soon brings the rudd into open water where they will feed ravenously. A biscuit hooked to a size 12 and cast with the aid of a controller float, should soon be taken. Do not strike when the bait is first taken: wait until the float begins to move away and the bait is well in the mouth.

Tip for the month
A little flavouring added to the *Chum* dog biscuits drives rudd wild. While the biscuits are soaking, add a little sweet flavouring to the water: maple, pineapple and strawberry all work well.

September

The carp is everybody's favourite fish, but for the very best of the year's sport it pays to wait until late summer. September is the month for very big fish, perhaps because the waters are quieter then, and the larger fish sense the approach of winter and the need to put on weight. Whatever the reason, September is the month when really big fish lose their wariness and become a little more vulnerable, both on the top and on the bottom.

All the usual summer methods and baits work quite well. September still offers excellent night fishing and dawn is frequently very productive. As the month progresses, the natural larder of food in the water begins to dwindle a little and anglers' baits become even more attractive. The last ten days of the month can be very rewarding.

Tip for the month
The majority of carp these days are caught on boilies, but remember that the humble lobworm used to be the favourite bait. Carp still love them, and as worms are little used now, the carp have little or

An ideal spot for carp — everybody's favourite fish.

A perch weighing 2 lbs, is a lovely fish – but they don't have to be this big to be an achievement.

no suspicion of them. Put two big worms on a size 4 for the best results.

OCTOBER

I have no doubt that barbel will be the cult fish of the 1990s. The enormous interest in them now is growing season by season. Furthermore, almost every angler lives within reach of these splendid river fish. East Anglia has the Wensum; for Londoners there is the Thames and, along the south coast, the Avon and Stour are probably the finest barbel waters in Britain. Yorkshire barbelling is first-rate while the area west of the Pennines has the Dane and the Ribble, both excellent barbel waters. In the West Midlands runs the brilliant Severn and, more centrally, everyone longs to fish the Kennet. Then, for anyone wanting a real challenge, there is the lure of the Wye.

The popularity of barbel is easy to explain. Their fight is the most dynamic of any British freshwater fish. There is a magic in the first run of the barbel that no carp or tench can equal and, even when that is finally subdued, the angler cannot relax until the fish is in the net.

The barbel feeds on the bottom of quick currents over clean gravel beds and that is where you must hunt it, either with big baits like luncheon meat or with particles such as sweetcorn and maggots. Most anglers ledger, but float fishing is more exciting and more productive. Barbel often prefer a moving bait and to see one on the gravel bed as it turns to intercept the bait is electrifying. The float disappears, you strike and the fun begins.

Tip for the month
Probably the very best time for barbel is during the first major floods of the year which often occur in October. Do not worry that water visibility is only a few inches; use a big strong-smelling bait, such as meat or cheese, and ledger it in a slack close to the bank.

NOVEMBER

For many years perch fishing was in decline. Nearly twenty years ago disease hit English perch stocks and water after water was cruelly struck as fine fish appeared ulcerated and dying. Now, at last, it seems that the disease is on the wane and, all over England, waters are recovering with staggering results. Big perch are being taken from rivers like the Wye and Trent, from reservoirs like Bewl Bridge and Ardleigh, and from pits and ponds just about everywhere. For the first time in two decades perching looks rosy.

Late autumn has always been the favoured time for perch. Weed is dying away then and the shoals of small fish are much easier to hunt. The perch gather into shoals and, if the angler finds one, then glorious sport can come his way. Scattering small fish is the tell-tale sign, especially a single fish skitting over the surface pursued by an ever-approaching bow-wave. Such a sight means perch, and offers the signal to get your bait in the water fast.

Small livebaits are favoured, but a fresh-killed deadbait is a close second. Roach, dace and gudgeon are all excellent baits. Big lobworms are in third place, while plugs and spinners are a poor, equal fourth. Maggots and even boilies have scored, but best of all is a small fish presented just off bottom, under a float. I hook them by a small treble in the mouth and strike soon after the run begins. A perch can engulf a bait in seconds and a deep-hooked perch is invariably a dead perch: something nobody wants.

Tip for the month
Perch hunt mainly by sight, but I am sure that sound and vibration also play their part. Very often I have had a perch run immediately after casting, so the lesson here is not to leave a bait out too long, but to move it fairly frequently.

DECEMBER

There is no other way to end the coarse fishing season than with pike, the most famous of coarse fish. River, lake, pond, pit, mere, broad or reservoir; all have their

THE COARSE FISHING YEAR

pike. How you fish them is your own concern, but remember that dawn and dusk are prime times; in clear water livebaits work best, whilst in cloudy water, deadbaits score.

Pike are a sadly abused species. Some anglers still wait painfully long before striking and hooks that are well down are hooks difficult to free. Other anglers are afraid of the pike on the bank and unhooking then becomes a farcical busines. Lay the pike on its back and, with gloved hand, pull its mouth open from the jawbone. It will lie still before you and allow the forceps to get to work on hooks that *must* be unbarbed. Everyone has the right to catch pike, but they must swim away unharmed after their ordeal.

History is full of tales of monster pike, and there are still huge fish to be caught. Trout reservoirs have a marvellous record of big fish. The Scottish and Irish lochs hold leviathans. Estate lakes and big pits all throw up large fish; the Norfolk Broads still hold thirty- and forty-pounders (13.6 – 18 kg), just waiting to be caught.

Tip for the month
Lure fishing for pike is becoming steadily more popular and a whole range of plugs and spinners is now available to the pike angler. However, choose lures carefully. Ask the tackle dealer which ones will best suit the type of water you are fishing. With a price tag up to £6 each, mistakes can be costly.

Fishing for pike, the most famous of coarse fish (above and opposite).

THE FISHERMAN'S YEARBOOK — THE COARSE FISHING YEAR

Pike Fishing
by Ken Whitehead

Pike are probably the most sought after fish in the British Isles today. Fishing for the species has steadily increased over the years and the sport is now under considerable pressure from the sheer numbers of rods which create overcrowding along popular fisheries and produce an extreme wariness among feeding fish. In both size (up to 45 lb (20 kg)) and fight, the species bring instant reward, while the extreme conditions under which the sport is practised, largely through the winter months, bring a challenge of their own.

Most pike anglers concentrate on fishing large waters such as lakes and reservoirs, particularly those waters opened in recent years by game anglers for pike to be culled. Equal sport, however, may be enjoyed in small waters, often mere ditches and ponds, which tend to be overlooked or incorrectly fished.

Folklore has decreed the pike to be a lazy fish, seeking holes and corners in slack water where it waits for small fish to present themselves as food. This is not true. Pike are equally at home in fast water and are capable of hunting for fish when hungry, although they do not kill for sport as does the otter. There is no established feeding pattern for pike, although anglers favour dawn and dusk as fishing times. It is also possible to stimulate fish into feeding by constantly presenting a bait or lure in front of them. During periods of extreme cold, pike tend to lie torpid, the inclination to feed falling with the temperature.

In recent years a tackle cult has grown around the pike with multiple types of rigs, specialist rods, advanced float designs and specially designed lures being held vital to success. While many of these innovations will occasionally result in a fish being taken during difficult times or circumstances, reliable tackle of good quality and basic design, together with intelligence, will suffice for most pike days and waters.

A rod in the 10–11 ft (3–3.3 m) range in glass-fibre, carbon-fibre or any modern derivative, capable of handling baits up to 4 oz (113g) or so, together with a skirted fixed-spool reel running on ball-bearings, will enable you to fish with both dead and livebaits, as well as spinning and plug fishing. Most anglers are catholic in their choice of line strength. Breaking strains should be matched

Some of the varied equipment available (above and opposite)

THE FISHERMAN'S YEARBOOK — PIKE FISHING — 19

more to weight of bait or lure to be cast and the action of the rod, than to the size of the expected catch.

More fish are landed during the course of the season using a Jardine snap-tackle rig than most other rigs put together. They are easily made using fine-cabled Alasticum or steel wire and small-sized fine wire hooks. There is a strong school supporting barbless hooks, or those with the incurve of the barb crushed, making for easier and safer unhooking. Most angling books stress the importance of a sharpening stone for hooks, although few, other than expert anglers, use one.

Livebaiting has always been the traditional method of taking pike, but there is now a gradual shift away from this style both on the grounds of cruelty and the risk of introducing unwanted species or disease into coarse and game fisheries. Deadbaits are finding increasing favour, either freshwater baits that have been frozen or sea species such as herring or mackerel. The old adage that the bigger the bait the bigger the fish is not necessarily true. Many 30lb-plus (13.6 kg) fish have been taken on a small sprat. Presentation matters far more than size.

Floatfishing is the most popular

The fleet in preparation (opposite) and a fine catch (left).

# PIKE FISHING

21

Fishing for pike (above) can produce impressive results (opposite).

method for livebaiting, using a float designed to give little or no resistance when towed by a taking fish. The float also features in deadbaiting, a recent innovation being the use of a sail mounted on the float-top so that the wind will carry part-floating baits into places where a cast cannot be made. Paternostering, where a bait is anchored in one place, either with or without the use of a float, is best for waters where drift from current or wind moves a bait away from the chosen fishing areas. Paternostering also ensures that a bait is kept at an established taking depth. Ledgering allows a bait to be fished at long distances as well as allowing a fish to pick up, without line or trace rising vertically above the bait. A sensitive bite indicator is a worthwhile investment and can be used with any of the three styles described above.

Pike seize any but the smallest of baits across the body, turning it to be swallowed headfirst. The saying, 'wait until the bait is turned before striking,' is slowly fading out, most anglers now striking earlier to prevent deep-hooking. There are a number of hook rigs that have been designed to function successfully with early hooking, but they are no substitute for commonsense.

Hooking is immediate when using a spinner or plug. Of the host of spinners available, the plain copper and silver spoon, mackerel spinner and leaf spinner in varying sizes will cover most waters and attract most pike. Multi-coloured spinners and those painted with a fish design disappear into a blur once the spinner revolves at speed. More important is establishing a taking depth, something which is best achieved by counting down after the spinner has landed and before it is retrieved.

Plugs are designed to work at varying depths and, again, simple is often best. Single bodies, naturally painted, without a profusion of hooks are the most successful. Deep-running for deep water, semi-floating for snag-infested fisheries where stopping, then retrieving, will allow the plug to rise to the surface and be eased into safety, are among the two best items for the tackle box.

It is always worth remembering that a suitable deadbait slowly retrieved and allowed to 'wobble' is cheaper and often more killing than the most expensive and well-designed artificial bait.

An extra-large landing net, disgorgers, forceps or long-nosed pliers are necessary to land and release fish, and ten minutes watching an expert releasing a badly-hooked pike will avoid a lifetime of bungling.

Country Code For Anglers

Respect for the environment, whether in the country or on the shore, is essential. The following rules of conduct should always be observed in order to protect your fishing and that of others, as well as that of fish and other forms of natural life.

● **Where stiles are provided use them.** Never climb or damage fences, hedges or walls. They are there to protect livestock. Keep to the path when approaching any fishery and avoid trampling grass, crops and wild flowers.

● **Close any gate you use.** If you must climb a gate, do so at the hinged end.

● **Never leave litter.** Apart from being unsightly, discarded litter can harm or even kill livestock, wild animals and birds. For the same reason never leave nylon line, hooks, especially baited hooks, shot or any other item of fishing tackle on the bankside or shore. Take them away for disposal.

● **Guard against the risk of fire.** Remember many fisheries ban the lighting of fires.

● **Keep dogs under control.** Many fisheries prohibit the presence of dogs.

● **Avoid contact with farm animals** and land on which animals are grazing.

● **Do not use transistor radios.** Most anglers detest them and many clubs prohibit their use.

● **Do not position yourself close to another angler's patch** and never, if at all avoidable, cast into another angler's swim.

● **Handle with care** fish you intend to return to the water. Never overcrowd fish in nets. Use a spacious keepnet (many fisheries stipulate mesh size and ring diameter) and wet your hands when handling fish to avoid damaging a fish's protective slime.

● **Report distressed fish.** A fish in distress is usually the victim of pollution, so report it to the local authority (Water Authority in England and Wales) as soon as possible.

● **Never kill undersize fish.** Where fisheries impose size limits, you must observe them.

● **Drive carefully** on country roads and observe any parking restrictions.

Active Carp Fishing
by Chris Yates

Carp fishers can be divided into two basic types; the active angler and the static, or armchair, angler. The active type uses his experience, imagination and intuition to catch carp. He is more interested in finding the fish than waiting for fish to find him. The armchair angler spends as much time observing the water as the active angler, but as his style of fishing is not so demanding, he has less need to be imaginative or intuitive. He likes to set up stall at a convenient spot and fish there for the duration, hoping to lure carp to him by generous (sometimes over-generous) offerings of groundbait.

Both anglers catch fish, but because the active angler often discovers carp feeding where the armchair angler fears to tread — in dense reed beds, under overhanging trees, by lily thickets — he enjoys more consistent success. The exception occurs when a group of hungry carp happen upon the armchair angler's bait. Then, because he is fishing a more 'comfortable' and, therefore, more open swim, he is often able to extract more fish than the active type could in his more restricted, secluded swims.

Having fished in the armchair style as well as in the manner of a stalking heron, I would say that, whatever happens, the active angler enjoys himself more. There is more variety to fishing because it demands a more flexible approach; it is more interesting because he never knows exactly how and where he is going to fish until he gets to the water, and, because he is looking for signs of feeding fish, he won't waste time fishing when he sees that the carp are unresponsive. Always watching and creeping quietly round the banks, he witnesses more of the carp's natural behaviour; close observation of your quarry is the best way to learn about it.

It seems nowadays that the great majority of carp anglers prefer the armchair method. This is a pity because there is a danger that they will become stereotyped in their thinking and mechanical in their fishing. Once that happens their favourite pastime can soon become unexciting, even boring. Active carp fishing can never be unexciting or boring because the situations you find yourself in can be full or surprises, like when you have crept stealthily along a screen of reeds and, on parting two stems, find yourself face to face with a monster carp.

I know many carp waters where armchair fishing is actually encouraged, where there are regimented, specially-constructed pitches and where bankside cover is regarded as an unnecessary evil. At these unfortunate places there is little potential for stalking and general creeping about, but nevertheless it is still worthwhile, especially on days when a strong, warm wind pushes the carp into specific areas close to the bank.

By 'active' fishing I do not mean that the angler is constantly flitting from swim to swim. He may decide to try a place where he feels a big carp may visit, even though there are no outward signs. He may wait silently for hours but, always alert, he is ready to alter his method instantly if it becomes evident that a carp is there and his presentation is wrong.

Let me give an example. A good friend of mine, Bob James, once had a look at a water that was producing some good carp. He wasn't interested in fishing on that first visit; he merely wished to investigate. He walked round the banks and immediately felt himself drawn to a deep channel between the two main pools of the lake. The channel was overhung with a large tree and Bob felt certain that carp might pause there and feed on their way from one pool to the other. He did not fish it until much later in the season, in late October, when the enthusiasm of the regular anglers had lessened and he had the lake more or less to himself.

Using the simplest of tackle – an 11 ft (3.3 m) split cane rod, centre pin reel, 6 lb line and size 6 hook – he cast a freelined flavoured paste bait under the leaning tree. He then scattered a few free offerings around it. His instinct for a good swim proved itself splendidly, for he caught three twenty-pounders (9 kg) carp in consecutive casts.

My own experiences have convinced me that quiet stalking round a carp pool, one that is fairly natural with plenty of trees and bankside vegetation, is the most exciting and rewarding method of catching carp. To demonstrate that this method so often has the advantage over

Chris Yates with a double-figure common carp.

the static approach, let me relate a typical incident. After a fortnight's drought, a sudden, prolonged downpour soaked the landscape putting fresh water into streams, re-oxygenating ponds and lakes and revitalising previously lethargic carp. When the rain stopped, I grabbed a rod, net and baitbox and set off, full of confidence, to a favourite carp pond.

As expected, the carp were making themselves obvious, swimming enthusiastically between the weed and lily beds, looking eager to snatch the first bait they saw. I merely had to creep along between the bankside trees, until I found one within easy casting range.

I passed two carp anglers, who had just arrived, unloading a vast amount of tackle and equipment in preparation for a serious night session in a big, open swim. Before they had even made up their rods, I caught a double-figure common carp. It had taken a single *Chum* dog biscuit freelined on a size 8 hook, close into the margins. By the time the two anglers had cast out I had caught another double-figure fish, this time by dropping a maple-flavoured peanut into a patch of bubbles. Although I was sure I could have caught more, I left the water and went home for supper. Returning the next morning, I found the two anglers about to give up after a fruitless night. I persuaded them to go for an exploratory search round the banks, taking with them simply a rod, net and bag of bait – *my* bag of bait!

Carp activity had lessened a good deal since the previous evening but, by careful observation, they discovered two or three nice fish feeding on the bottom, sending up tell-tale streams of bubbles. The result was a double-figure carp apiece and two more converts to the active school of carp fishing.

The Water Authorities Of England And Wales

In England and Wales the Water Authorities are government-appointed bodies that exist to control the use of freshwater for all sections of the community. These include, primarily and essentially, agriculture and industry, important water-users whose interests must inevitably conflict at times to a greater or lesser degree with those of sporting enthusiasts. An example is the contentious matter of water abstraction for agriculture. The Hampshire Avon has suffered particularly in this respect, but only so far as the angler is concerned. The farmer's legitimate needs for use of the river's water in irrigation and so on must be paramount over any sporting interest, but try convincing anglers of this when a particularly prolific stretch of chub water suddenly falls below the level necessary to hold the fish.

The sporting factions include angling, sailing, canoeing, pleasure-cruising, rowing, power-boat racing, water-skiing, diving, bird-watching, shooting, all of which can have a legitimate interest in, and right to share, the liquid amenity of freshwater. It is inevitable, too, that these sporting interests will come into conflict, and one faction or another will make dogmatic statements and claims that their 'right' should have precedence over another's. Clearly, someone has to sort it out. Many an angler has had to reel in quickly before a badly-skippered dinghy carries his terminal tackle away; on the other hand, that same skipper might well have been bombarded with ledger weights while blissfully sailing where he was entitled to!

Once called River Boards, the Water Authorities were formed in line with the Water Act 1973, and the Salmon and Freshwater Fisheries Act 1975. So far as angling is concerned, Water Authorities govern the way fishing is carried out in freshwaters everywhere in England and Wales. Scotland has different bodies which control, the use of water as an amenity. The ten Water Authorities, which liaise with the National Water Council, decide on the cost of fishing licences for the rivers and still waters under their control; the acceptable methods of fishing and the size limits below which fish must be returned to the water; impose and regulate the close seasons, as well as conservancy measures such as imposing minimum mesh sizes, material and ring diameters of keepnets.

Before fishing in England and Wales, the angler must be in possession of the fishing licence appropriate to the water he intends to fish; he must also have permission, usually obtained by payment of a fee or through membership of a club or body which controls the water. There are very few free fisheries these days and any visiting angler should ask at tackle shops for information about local fishing.

Pollution

Pollution of freshwater has been an increasing problem for many years, caused mainly by farming slurry and insecticides or toxic and harmful wastes from industry. Of course, this pollution is an offence and there is legal machinery, in the shape of the Control of Pollution Act 1974, to prevent or stop it. But the litigation necessary to prove harmful pollution can be prolonged and costly, one reason being that if forced to stop serious pollution, a company might be financially crippled or its production reduced so severely that its profitability will be threatened. It thus has a strong case, the pollution notwithstanding, for defending its position and invariably does so. Even so, the Water Authorities, the National Anglers' Council and the Anglers' Co-operative Association have all, at times, brought a case against pollution to a successful conclusion, but it is not a matter for the individual unless he has very large financial resources.

PRIVATISATION

There are now government moves to privatise the Water Authorities, with private bodies adopting the responsibilities of the present Authorities, £7 billion being suggested as a flotation figure. The price of shares in the twenty-eight private statutory water companies has already risen tenfold in twelve months. Speaking for the country's three-million-plus anglers, the National Anglers' Council has voiced doubts that unless stringent safeguards are included in any legislation, fishing interests may be at risk. Anglers feel that privatisation may well lead to overt interest in the profitability avenues of water usage, to the detriment of fisheries and sportfishing. The vexed question of the cost of rod licences in many areas has suggested that a single, national licence may be a good idea, but this highly complex matter is a long way from being understood, let alone resolved to the satisfaction of all.

Editor's Note
Current privatisation proposals aim at creating a new National Rivers' Authority to take over from the existing Water Authorities' responsibilities for the protection of rivers, pollution, water abstraction and other regulatory functions. When the Water Bill becomes law, which it may in 1989, anglers will have to direct their problems to the new National Rivers' Authority. Although reorganisation is likely sometime in 1989, its consequences to the information given cannot be predicted at this stage. Anglers are advised to contact their local Water Authority head office (with the exception of South West Water where the new NRA address is given) listed in this guide for further information.

National Rivers' Authority is the name currently being used for the new body. It may, however, change.

The River Dart.

The Water Authorities of England and Wales

ANGLIAN WATER

Chief Estates, Recreation and Conservation: Douglas Dent.
Regional Scientist (Environment and Fisheries): Ron Linfield.
Ambury Road,
Huntingdon,
Cambs PE18 6NZ.
Tel: Huntingdon (0480) 56181.

Pollution Control
Report to the Regional Scientist or the 24-hour emergency number: Norwich 761761

Close Seasons
SALMON, SEA TROUT, BROWN AND RAINBOW TROUT (not in enclosed water): 29 September – 28/29 February
BROWN AND RAINBOW TROUT (enclosed waters): 30 October – 31 March (inclusive).
COARSE FISH AND EELS: 15 March – 15 June (inclusive)

Licences
SALMON, TROUT, FRESHWATER FISH AND EELS: Regional annual licence (valid anywhere within the Anglian Water Authority boundary) £7.50.
Regional 7 day licence: £1.50.
Regional concessionary annual licence (juveniles 12–15 years inclusive; senior citizens; registered disabled): £2.50.
A licence is not required for fishing eels in tidal waters downstream of points scheduled in Fishery Bye-laws.

Divisional licences are to be discontinued in 1989.

Divisional Offices

Cambridge Division
Biological Services Officer: Pat Noble,
Great Ouse House,
Clarendon Road,
Cambridge CB2 2BL.
Tel: Cambridge (0223) 61561.

Colchester Division
Fisheries Scientist:
Robin Burrough,
33 Sheepen Road,
Colchester CO3 3LB.
Tel: Colchester (0206) 763344.

Lincoln Division
Fisheries and Conservation Scientist:
Tim Coles,
Waterside House,
Waterside North,
Lincoln LN2 5HA.
Tel: Lincoln (0522) 25231.

Norwich Division
Fisheries Scientist:
Jonathan Wortley
Yare House,
62/64 Thorpe Road,
Norwich NR1 1SA.
Tel: Norwich (0603) 615161.

Oundle Division
Fisheries Scientist: Peter Barham,
North Street,
Oundle,
Peterborolugh PE8 4AS.
Tel: Peterborough (0832) 73701.

THAMES WATER

Customer Services Officer:
Colin Millikin.
Nugent House,
Vastern Road,
Reading,
Berkshire RG1 8DB.
Tel: Reading (0734) 593777/593333

Upper Thames
David Jenkins
Thames Water,
Denton House,
Iffley Road,
Oxford OX4 4HJ.
Tel: Oxford (0865) 778921

Middle Thames
Alan Butterworth,
Thames Water,
Ladymead,
Bypass Road,
Guildford,
Surrey GU1 1BZ.
Tel: Guildford (0483) 577655

Thames East
John Reeves,
Thames Water,
Aspen House,
The Grange,
Crossbrook Street,
Waltham Cross,
Herts EN8 8LX
Tel: Waltham Cross (0992) 23611

Metropolitan
Steve Colclough,
Rivers Division,
Crossness STW,
Abbey Wood,
London SE2 9AQ.
Tel: 01 310 5500.

THE FISHERMAN'S YEARBOOK   WATER AUTHORITIES   31

Pollution Control
Cases of pollution should be reported by dialling 100 and asking for Thames Water FREEFONE 3266. This is a 24-hour, seven-days-a-week service.

Close Seasons
SALMON AND TROUT (exluding rainbow trout): period between 30 September and 1 April except any enclosed reservoir, lake or pond fishing for trout 29 October and 1 April.
RAINBOW TROUT: 30 September and 1 April (does not apply to enclosed waters).
COARSE: period between 14 March and 16 June.
EELS: 14 March and 16 June except in tidal River Thames downstream of the Thames Barrier, no close season.

Licences
Note that all licences expire 31 March following date of issue.. Annual full £7.50; senior citizens, registered disabled and juniors (12–16) £2. 15-day £2.

Divisional Offices

Rivers Division
Thames Water,
Nugent House,
Vastern Road,
Reading RG1 8DB.

Central Division
Thames Water,
Roseberry Avenue,
New River Head,
London EC1R 4TP.

East & North Division
Aspen House,
The Grange,
Crossbrook Street,
Waltham Cross,
Herts EN8 8LX.

South & West Division
Thames Water,
c/o Nugent House,
Vastern Road,
Reading RG1 8DB.

SOUTHERN WATER

Regional Fisheries Officer:
Mr J. Chandler,
Guildbourne House,
Chatsworth Road,
Worthing,
West Sussex.
Tel: Worthing (0903) 205252.

Pollution Control
Contact the appropriate Rivers Division Office
Isle of Wight: Newport (0983) 526611 during office hours; Sandown (0983) 2106 at other times.
Hampshire: Twyford (0962) 714585.
Sussex: Brighton (0273) 606766.
Kent: Medway (0634) 830655.

Close Seasons
SALMON: the period between 2 October and 17 January.
MIGRATORY TROUT: the period between 31 October and 1 May.
NON-MIGRATORY TROUT (inc. rainbow): the period between 31 October and 3 April. No close season for rainbow trout in enclosed reservoirs, lakes and ponds containing rainbow trout only.
COARSE: statutory.

Licences
SALMON (inc. trout, coarse and eels): annual £30; 14 day £10; day £5.
MIGRATORY TROUT (inc. non-migratory trout, coarse and eels): annual £5; 28 day £2.50; Junior (under 16) annual £2.50.
COARSE AND EELS ONLY: Senior citizens and disabled free.

Area offices

Hampshire & IOW
Hampshire Fishery Officer:
Mr R. Crawshaw,
SWA, Otterbourne,
Winchester,
Hampshire.
Tel: Twyford (0962) 714585.

Sussex
Sussex Fisheries Officer:
Dr B. Buckley,
SWA, Falmer, Brighton, East Sussex.
Tel: Brighton (0273) 606766.

Kent
Kent Fisheries Officer:
SWA, Mr K. Wilson,
Luton House,
Capstone Road,
Chatham,
Kent.
Tel: Medway (0634) 830655.

WESSEX WATER

Chief Fisheries and Recreational Officer:
A. J. R. Barber,
Wessex House,
Passage Street,
Bristol BS2 0JQ.
Tel: Bristol (0272) 290611.

Pollution Control
Contact the appropriate Divisional Office during office hours or the following 24-hour emergency service numbers:
Bristol Avon Division 0345 078 505.
Avon & Dorset Division: 0345 078 515.
Somerset Division: 0345 078 535.

Close Seasons
SALMON: Period between 30 September and 1 February, except in the Rivers Frome and Piddle (Avon & Dorset Division) where the close season period is between 30 September and 1 March.

MIGRATORY TROUT: period between 31 October and 15 April.
NON-MIGRATORY TROUT (inc. rainbow trout): period between 15 October and 1 April except the River Avon above the Mill Dam at Bicton Mill. (This does not include the River Nadder above the road bridge at Barford St Martin). Reservoirs, lakes and ponds – the period between 15 October and 17 March. There is no close season for rainbow trout in reservoirs, lakes and ponds containing rainbow trout only.
COARSE AND EELS: period between 14 March and 16 June.

Licences
SALMON (inc. trout, coarse and eels): annual £25, concessionary (juniors 12–16 years, senior citizens and registered disabled) £12.50; week £4, concessionary £2.
TROUT (inc. sea trout, rainbow trout, coarse and eels): annual £8.20, concessionary £4.10; week £2, concessionary £1.
COARSE AND EELS: annual £6.35, concessionary £3.15; week £1.55, concessionary 75p.

Divisional Offices
Bristol Avon Division
Divisional Fisheries and Recreational Officer:
Mr Adrian Taylor,
Quay House,
PO Box 95,
The Ambury
Bath BA1 2YP.
Tel: Bath (0225) 313500.

Avon & Dorset Division
Divisional Fisheries and Recreational Officer:
Dr Duncan Wilkinson,
2 Nuffield Road,
Poole,
Dorset BH17 7RL.
Tel: Poole (0202) 671144.

Somerset Division
Divisional Fisheries and Recreational Officer:
Mr C. Arden,
PO Box 9,
King Square,
Bridgwater,
Somerset TA6 3EA.
Tel: (0278) 457333.

SOUTH WEST WATER

Recreations Officer: Stuart Bray,
Peninsula House,
Rydon Lane,
Exeter EX2 7HR.
Tel: Exeter (0392) 219666.

After privatisation the headquarters of the new National Rivers' Authority will be at:
Manley House,
Kestrel Way,
Exeter EX2 7LQ.
Tel: Exeter (0392) 76201.
The persons responsible for fishing under the NRA are already at this address and any enquiries about river fishing should be addressed to either Dr B. R. Merry or Mr G. D. Eames.

The existing Recreation Section, responsible for still water and reservoir fisheries, will, however, remain with the Water Authority PLC at the address given above. For information about reservoir fishing (coarse and game) contact either head office or the Area Ranger.

RECREATION RANGERS
East Cornwall
Ranger: Reg England,
Tregarrick Lodge,
Siblyback Lake,
Liskeard.
Tel: Liskeard (0579) 42366.
Reservoirs: Crafthold, Colliford, Crowdy, Siblyback.

Exmoor
Ranger: Bob Lunk,
Hill Farm,
Brompton Regis,
Dulverton.
Tel: Dulverton (0398) 7372
Reservoirs/Rivers: Slade, Wimbleball Lake, River Lyn, Glenthorne and Watersmeet fishery.

North West Devon
Ranger: Ken Spalding,
Sparrapark,
Kilkhampton,
Bude.
Tel: Bude (0288) 2262
Reservoirs: Darracott, Gammaton, Jennetts, Melbury, Tamar Lakes.

West Cornwall
Ranger: Bob Evans,
Little Argal Farm,
Budock,
Penryn.
Tel: Falmouth (0326) 72544.
Reservoirs: Argal, Boscathnoe, Bussow, College, Drift, Porth, Stithians.

Dartmoor
Ranger: Russell Stevens,
Metherall Cottage,
Chagford.
Tel: Chagford (06473) 2440.
Reservoirs/Rivers: Avon Dam, Burrator, Butterbrook, Fernworthy, Kennick/Tottiford/Trenchford, Meldon, Old Mill, Venford, River Dart and Buckfastleigh fishery.

Pollution Control
Report suspected pollution by telephoning the office for the area in which the pollution has occurred:
Exeter (0392) 76201

SOUTH-WEST WATER OPEN SEASONS

Species Fish	Fishery District	Major Rivers within District	Rod & Line Open Season (dates inc.)	
			Commences	Finishes
Salmon	Avon	Avon	15 Apr	30 Nov E
		Erme	15 Mar	31 Oct
	Axe	Axe, Lim, Otter, Sid	15 Mar	31 Oct
	Camel	Camel	1 April	15 December
	Dart	Dart	1 Feb	30 Sept E
	Exe	Exe	14 Feb	30 Sept
	Fowey	Fowey, Looe, Seaton	1 Apr	15 Dec
	Tamar & Plym	Tamar, Tavy, Lynher	1 Mar	14 Oct
		Plym	1 Apr	15 Dec
		Yealm	1 Apr	15 Dec E
	Taw & Torridge	Taw, Torridge	1 Mar	30 Sept
		Lyn	1 Feb	31 Oct
	Teign	Teign	1 Feb	30 Sept*
Migratory Trout	Avon	Avon	15 Apr	30 Sept
		Erme	15 Mar	30 Sept
	Axe	Axe, Lim, Otter, Sid	15 Apr	31 Oct
	Camel	Camel, Gannel, Menalhyl Valency	1 Apr	30 Sept
	Dart	Dart	15 Mar	30 Sept
	Exe	Exe	15 Mar	30 Sept
	Fowey	Fowey, Looe, Seaton, Tresillian	1 Apr	30 Sept
	Tamar & Plym	Tamar, Lynher, Plym, Tavy, Yealm	3 Mar	30 Sept
	Taw & Torridge	Taw, Torridge, Lyn	15 Mar	30 Sept
	Teign	Teign, Bovey	15 Mar	12 Oct
Brown Trout	Entire Region	R. Camel & R. Fowey	1 Apr	30 Sept
		Other Rivers & Streams	15 Mar	30 Sept
		All Other Waters	15 Mar	12 Oct
Rainbow Trout	ENTIRE REGION		NO CLOSE SEASON	
Coarse Fish	ENTIRE REGION		NO CLOSE SEASON	

* Between 1–30 September inclusive each angler is allowed a limit of two fish in total. Some owners or clubs with fishing rights do impose their own close season dates within the above periods.

Paignton (0803) 556281
Barnstable (0271) 76126
Launceston (064 45) 2151
Truro (0872) 76131
Bodmin (0208) 5777
Outside office hours dial 100 and ask the operator for FREEFONE 920. This is a 24-hour service.

Open Seasons
(see chart)

Licences
Rod licences are for the period 1 Jan – 31 Dec. At the time of going to press, 1989 prices were not available.

Area Officials

T. Ford,
SWW,
Pilton West,
Barnstable,
Devon EX31 1TT.
Tel: Barnstable (0271) 76126.

D. K. Clifton,
SWW,
Kings Ash Road,
Paignton,
Devon TQ3 3XQ.
Tel: Paignton (0803) 556281.

NOTE: Some waters are not open for the full duration of the season, and anglers are advised to check with the fishery owner if in doubt. As part of the Authority's Strategy on Salmon Cropping, the season on some rivers has been changed experimentally and is indicated with an E.

B. R. Letts & T. Smith,
SWW,
Victoria Square,
Bodmin,
Cornwall PL31 1EB.
Tel: Bodmin (0208) 5777.

R. Rowledge,
SWW,
Southcott,
Chapple,
Launceston,
Cornwall.
Tel: Launceston (0566) 2151.

SEVERN-TRENT WATER

Regional Fisheries Officer:
P. Hickey,
Abelson House,
2297 Coventry Road,
Sheldon,
Birmingham B26 3PU.
Tel: Birmingham (021) 722 4000.

Pollution Control
Nottingham (0602) 608161.
Stoke (0782) 85601.
Derby (0332) 661481.
Tewkesbury (0684) 297187.
Shrewsbury (0743) 231666.
Leicester (0533) 352011.
Birmingham (021) 454 3503.
Coventry (0203) 22182.

Riverline: 24-hour telephone-answering service providing information on local river levels. Trench Catchment Area tel: (0898) 333911.

Avon and Lower Severn Area
tel: (0898) 333922.
Upper and Middle Severn Area
tel: (0898) 333933.

Close Seasons
SALMON: period between 30 September and 2 February.
MIGRATORY TROUT: period between 30 September and 16 March.
TROUT (excluding migratory and rainbow trout): in all waters in the Severn area the period between 30 September and 18 March, except in lakes and reservoirs in the Severn area and all water in the Trent area, the period between 15 October and 18 March.
RAINBOW TROUT: No close season in all waters in the Authority except in Rivers Derwent and Amber (inc. tributaries) upstream of their confluence (excluding the stretch between Blackwell Mill to Cressbrook Mill) and above Ashford on Derbyshire Wye, period between 15 November and 16 May.
COARSE: statutory.
EELS: No close season.

Licences
SALMON: annual £32.65, concessionary £6.55; 28 day £13.05; day £6.55.
TROUT, COARSE and EELS: annual* £4.50, concessionary 90p; 28 day* £1.80. *inc. salmon fishing in Trent area.

Divisional Offices
Northern Division
Fisheries Recreation Officer,
Severn-Trent Water,
Raynesway,
Derby DE2 7JA.
Tel: Derby (0332) 661481.

Southern Division
Fisheries Recreational Officer,
Seven-Trent Water,
De Montfort Way,
Cannon Park,
Coventry CV4 7EJ.
Tel: Coventry (0203) 416510.

Eastern Division
Fisheries Recreational Officer,
Severn-Trent Water,
Leicester Water Centre,
Gorse Hill,
Anstey,
Leicester LE7 7GU.
Tel: Leicester (0533) 352011.

Western Division
Fisheries Recreation Officer,
Severn-Trent Water,
Tame House,
156–170 Newhall Street,
Birmingham B3 1SE.
Tel: Birmingham (021) 200 2020.

YORKSHIRE WATER
Amenity Fisheries and Recreation Manager:
Dr D. J. Shillcock.
21 Park Square South, Leeds LS1 2QG
Tel: Leeds (0532) 440191
Pollution Control
Contact the Area Office (for addresses and telephone numbers see below) for the area where the pollution has occurred.

Close Seasons
SALMON AND SEA-TROUT: 1 November – 5 April (inclusive).
TROUT: 1 October – 24 March (inclusive).
COARSE and EELS: 28 February – 31 May.

Licences
SALMON, TROUT, COARSE and EELS throughout the Authority's area (inc. River Esk): season* £41.60, concessionary (juveniles 10–15 years, senior citizens and registered disabled) £20.80; 7 day £16.80, concessionary £8.40; day £8.40, concessionary £4.20.
COARSE (inc. salmon, trout and eels, except salmon and migratory trout in the Esk and its tributaries and streams to the north of the Esk): season* £5.20, concessionary £2.60; 7 day £2.10, concessionary £1.05.
*25 March 1988–24 March 1989.

Area Offices
North & East
Eric Gore-Browne,
Yorkshire Water,
32–34 Monkgate,
York.
Tel: York (0904) 642131.

Central
Janine Day,
Yorkshire Water,
Spenfield,
182 Otley Road,
Leeds.
Tel: Leeds (0532) 781313.

Western
David Milner,
Yorkshire Water,
Western House,
Halifax Road,
Bradford.
Tel: Bradford (0274) 691111.

Southern
John Howe,
Yorkshire Water,
Castle Market Building,
Exchange Street,
Sheffield.
Tel: Sheffield (0742) 726421.

NORTH WEST WATER
Head Office: Dawson House,
Great Sankey, Warrington
WA5 3LW.
Tel: Penketh (092572) 4321.

Regional Fisheries Officer:
C. Harpley,
PO Box 30,
New Town House,
Buttermarket Street,
Warrington WA1 2QG.
Tel: Warrington (0925) 53999.

Pollution Control

Rivers Ribble, Darwen, Lostock, Yarrow and northwards: Tel Carlisle (0228) 25151 during office hours.
Rivers Douglas, Irwell, Mersey and southwards: Tel: Warrington (0925) during office hours.
Other times tel: (061) 370 3155.

Close Seasons

SALMON: 1 November – 31 January except River Eden and all systems 15 October – 14 January.
MIGRATORY TROUT: 16 October – 30 April except Rivers Annas, Bleng, Cumbrian Esk, Mite Irt, Calder, Ehen and all their systems, 1 November – 30 April.
NON-MIGRATORY TROUT (except rainbow): 1 October – 14 march.
RAINBOW TROUT (rivers and streams): 1 October – 14 October. There is no close season for lakes, reservoirs and enclosed waters.
CHAR: 1 October – 14 March except Coniston Water (1 November – 14 March) when fishing with an artificial lure from a moving boat.
COARSE and EELS: 15 March – 15 June.

Licences

SALMON: annual £29, concessionary (junior 14–16 years, senior citizens and registered disabled) £14.50; part year £22, concessionary £11; week £7.
MIGRATORY TROUT: annual £12, concessionary £6; week £3.
BROWN, RAINBOW TROUT AND CHAR: annual £5, concessionary £2.50; week £1.75
COARSE AND EELS: annual £4, concessionary £2; week £1. Juniors under 14 do not require a licence. Salmon licences include all other categories; migratory trout licences include non-migratory trout, coarse and eels, non-migratory licences include coarse and eels.

Area Offices

North Area
District Fisheries Officer:
C. Newton,
Chertsey Hill,
London Road,
Carlisle CA1 2QX.
Tel: Carlisle (0228) 25151;

Central Area
District Fisheries Officer:
C. Durie,
Beathwaite,
Levens,
Kendal,
Cumbria LA8 8NL.
Tel: Sedgwick (05395) 60567.

South Area
District Fisheries Officer:
J. Leeming,
PO Box 30,
New Town House,
Buttermarket Street,
Warrington WA1 2QG.
Tel: Warrington (0925) 53999.

NORTHUMBRIAN WATER

Chief Fisheries Officer:
A. S. Champion,
PO Box 4,
Regent Centre,
Gosforth,
Newcastle-upon-Tyne NE3 3PX.
Tel: Tyneside (091) 284 3151.

Pollution Control

Telephone the above number or the appropriate area office in which the pollution occurs.

Close Seasons

SALMON: period between 31 October – 1 February.
MIGRATORY TROUT: period between 31 October – 3 April.
NON-MIGRATORY TROUT: period between 30 September – 23 March (exclusive) except Kielder Reservoir, 1 November – 30 April (inclusive).
COARSE AND EELS: statutory for rivers and streams; no close season for lakes, reservoirs or ponds.

Licences (for all waters in the Authority's area excluding the River Tweed and tributaries):

SALMON, MIGRATORY TROUT, TROUT, COARSE AND EELS: annual £41, concessionary (juveniles under 16 years, senior citizens and registered disabled) £20.60; 14 day £13; day £6.
TROUT (excluding migratory trout, coarse and eels): annual £10, concessionary £5; 14 days £3.80; day £1.
COARSE: annual £3.80, concessionary £1.90.
COARSE AND EELS: annual £4.

Area Offices

Northumberland & Tyne Division
Northumberland Water,
Northumbria House,
Town Centre,
Cramlington,
Northumberland NE23 6UP.
Tel: Cramlington (0670) 713322.

Wear Division
Northumberland Water,
Wear House,
Abbey Road,
Pity Me,
Durham DH1 5EZ.
Tel: Durham (091) 384 4222.

Tees Division
Northumberland Water,
Trenchard Avenue,
Thornaby,
Stockton-on-Tees TS17 0EQ.
Tel: Stockton (0642) 760216.

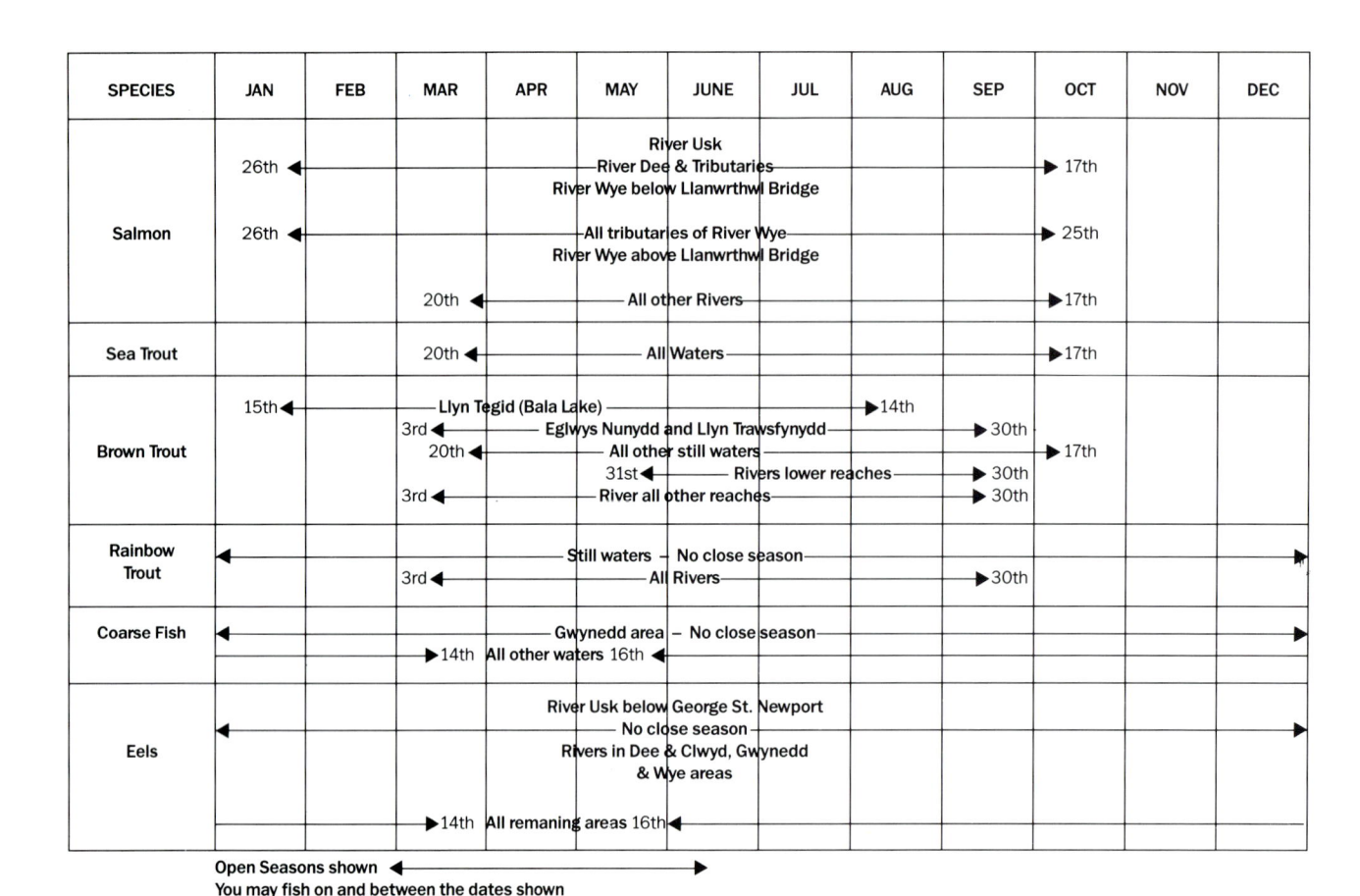

SPECIES	JAN	FEB	MAR	APR	MAY	JUNE	JUL	AUG	SEP	OCT	NOV	DEC
Salmon	26th ◀				River Usk — River Dee & Tributaries — River Wye below Llanwrthwl Bridge					▶ 17th		
	26th ◀				All tributaries of River Wye — River Wye above Llanwrthwl Bridge					▶ 25th		
			20th ◀		All other Rivers					▶ 17th		
Sea Trout			20th ◀		All Waters					▶ 17th		
Brown Trout	15th ◀		Llyn Tegid (Bala Lake)					▶ 14th				
			3rd ◀		Eglwys Nunydd and Llyn Trawsfynydd				▶ 30th			
			20th ◀		All other still waters				▶ 30th	▶ 17th		
					31st ◀	Rivers lower reaches			▶ 30th			
			3rd ◀		River all other reaches				▶ 30th			
Rainbow Trout	◀				Still waters — No close season							▶
			3rd ◀		All Rivers				▶ 30th			
Coarse Fish	◀				Gwynedd area — No close season							▶
			▶ 14th	All other waters 16th ◀								
Eels	◀				River Usk below George St. Newport — No close season — Rivers in Dee & Clwyd, Gwynedd & Wye areas							▶
			▶ 14th	All remaining areas 16th ◀								

Open Seasons shown ◀——▶
You may fish on and between the dates shown

WELSH WATER

Fisheries Officer:
John Gregg,
Plas y Ffynnon,
Brecon,
Powys LD3 7HP.
Tel: Brecon (0874) 3181.

Pollution Control
Telephone Brecon (0874) 3181.

Open Seasons
(see diagram)

Licences
SALMON AND MIGRATORY TROUT (inc. non-migratory trout, char, coarse fish and eels): full season £29.50, concessionary (juveniles 10–16 years inclusive, senior citizens, registered unemployed and disabled) £19.75; 14 days £13.75; day £5; special junior (covers all species and all areas available to children under 10) 80p.
NON-MIGRATORY TROUT (inc. brown and rainbow trout, char, coarse fish and eels): full season £8.50, concessionary £5.75; 14 day £2; day £1.65.
COARSE AND EELS: full season £5, concessionary £3.30. Welsh Water controls the fishing in over twenty reservoirs. Permit prices are published each year in January and may be obtained from: The Estates & Recreation Officer, Welsh Water, SE Division HQ, Pentwyn Road, Nelson, Treharris, Mid Glam CF46 6LY. Tel: (0443) 45077.

Area Offices

North Wales
District Fisheries Officer,
Welsh Water,
Penrhosgarnedd,
Bangor.
Tel: Bangor (0248) 351144.

South East Wales
District Fisheries Officer,
Welsh Water,
Pentwyn Road,
Nelson,
Mid Glam.
Tel: Nelson (0443) 450577.

South West Wales
District Fisheries Officer,
Welsh Water,
Hawthorne Rise,
Haverfordwest.
Tel: Haverfordwest (0437) 4581.

SCOTLAND

There are no Water Authorities in Scotland in the English sense. Regional Councils exist but their function extends to water supply only and does not include fisheries. There are no statutory bodies responsible for salmon and freshwater fisheries in Scotland. However, groups of proprietors may form District Fishery Boards endowed under the Salmon Fisheries (Scotland) Acts of 1862–68, with certain powers of enforcing the law and developing salmon fisheries, but these are voluntary bodies and do not exist over the whole country.

Trout fishing is also controlled by the Fishery Boards and riparian owners. Close seasons for both salmon and trout vary considerably between the various river systems and the statutory close season parameters. Rainbow trout in Scotland have no official close season, but authorities do exercise their rights by instituting their own close seasons. Few Scottish anglers will admit to the presence of coarse fish species in their waters, so no close season exists. However, visiting anglers should always check since owners can prohibit coarse fishing at certain times on their waters.

The overall jurisdiction of fishing in Scotland is administered by the Inspector of Salmon and Freshwater Fisheries, Department of Agriculture and Fisheries, Chesser House (Room 426), Gorgie Road, Edinburgh EH11 3AW. Tel: Edinburgh (031) 443 4020, ext 2190.

For information about fishing holidays in Scotland contact the Scottish Tourist Office, 23 Ravelston Terrace, Edinburgh EH4 3EU. Tel: 031-332 2433.

NORTHERN IRELAND

The body ultimately responsible for the administration of fisheries in Northern Ireland is the Department of Agriculture, Fisheries Division, Hut 5, Castle Grounds, Stormont, Belfast. There are, in addition, two other bodies working closely with the Department of Agriculture in the conservation and protection of fisheries, including pollution: the Foyle Fisheries Commission and The Fisheries Conservancy Board for Northern Ireland. These two bodies are responsible for different areas of the country.

Foyle Fisheries Commission
8 Victoria Road,
Londonderry BT47 2AB.
Tel: Londonderry (0504) 42100.
Information on angling in the area may be obtained from the Chief

WATER AUTHORITIES

Inspector at the above address and telephone number. The 0504 code is a UK one.

The Commission is responsible for conservation and protection of fisheries for an area which lies partly in Northern Ireland and partly in the Republic of Ireland. It includes the catchments of all rivers flowing into the sea between Malin Head, County Donegal, and Downhill, County Londonderry.

Angling is virtually all trout and sea trout and salmon in season – spring salmon on the River Finn from 1 March and summer salmon from mid-June throughout the Foyle area. There is also limited coarse fishing in the Omagh and Strabane/Lifford areas.

The waters controlled and covered by a Foyle Area Licence (but not necessarily owned by the Commission, thus permission to fish may also be required) are: the Rivers Foyle, Finn, Mourne, Derg, Owenkillew, Glenelly, Fairywater, Camowen, Drumragh, Faughan, Roe and Deele. Still waters: Loughs Ash, Alaan, Moor, Braden, Lee Binevenagh and Derg.

Glenelly Valley, Co. Tyrone

The Fisheries Conservancy Board for Northern Ireland,
1 Mahon Road,
Portadown,
County Armargh.

Close Seasons
SALMON, SEA TROUT, BROWN TROUT AND RAINBOW TROUT: Lough Foyle, River Foyle and River Finn (including the loughs and tributaries of the River Finn): 16 September to the last day of February, inclusive.
Binevenagh Dam (rainbow trout): 1 January to 31 January, inclusive.
All the loughs in the Foyle area: 21 October to last day of February, inclusive. All other rivers in the Foyle area: 21 October to 31 March, inclusive.
COARSE FISH: no close season.
EELS: 1 December to 31 April.

Licences (1988 prices)
GAME: Season £10.70; juvenile (under 18) £5.35; 14 day game £6.80.
A licence for coarse fishing is not required provided that the method used is unlikely to catch game and that any game fish caught are returned to the water at once.

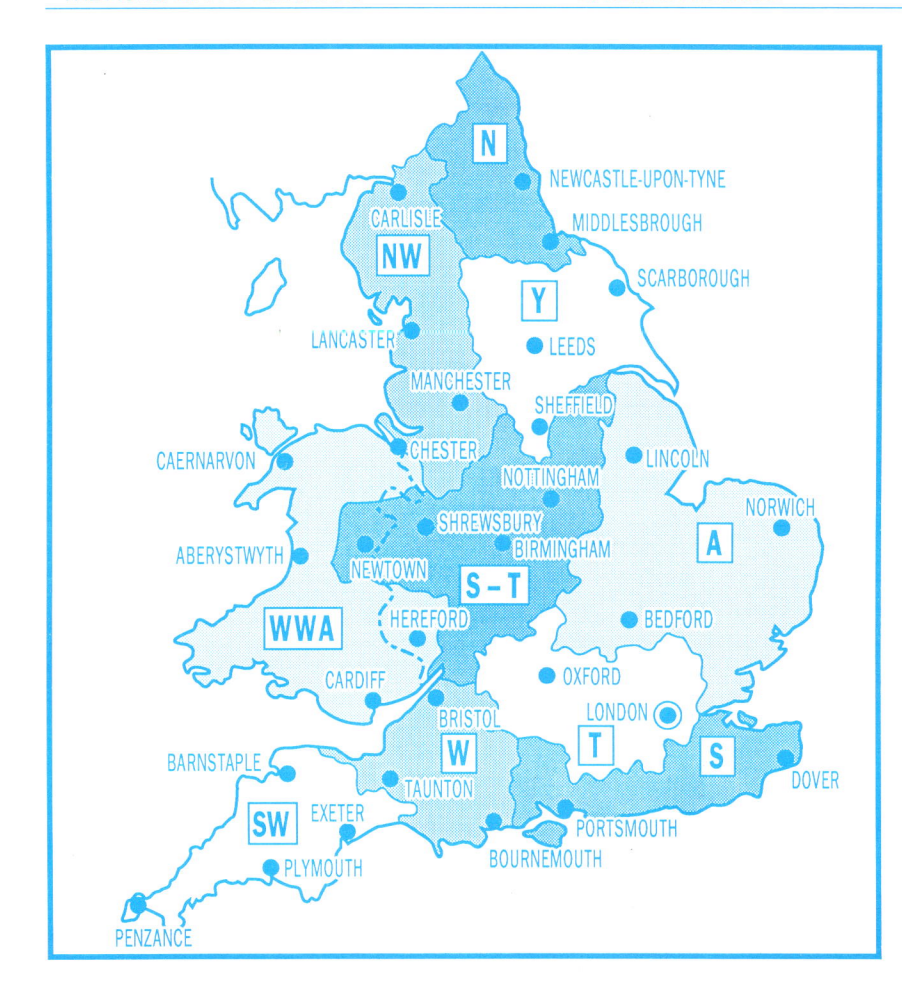

THE WATER AUTHORITIES OF ENGLAND AND WALES

KEY

- **A** Anglian Water Authority
- **T** Thames Water Authority
- **S** Southern Water Authority
- **W** Wessex Water Authority
- **SW** South West Water Authority
- **S-T** Severn-Trent Water Authority
- **Y** Yorkshire Water Authority
- **NW** North West Water Authority
- **N** Northumbrian Water Authority
- **WWA** Welsh Water Authority

THE GAME FISHING YEAR
by TREVOR HOUSBY

'To get the best out of modern trout fishing', writes Trevor Housby, 'the angler must fish month by month, taking into account the changes of nature and water conditions which, in turn, dictate the choice of flies and techniques employed.'

Traditionally, the trout fishers' year begins on 1 April or 1 May and finishes at the end of September. The salmon season starts a month earlier and ends a month sooner. Since the introduction of put-and-take fisheries, however, these traditional seasonal boundaries have changed and, in some instances, have vanished completely. Waters which stock only rainbow trout may now stay open twelve months of the year although mixed rainbow and brown trout fisheries generally follow the 1 April ruling. The reason for this is that rainbow trout are an introduced species which in Britain very rarely spawn in the wild. Brown trout, being a native species, can and do spawn naturally. Once spawning has been completed the fish must be given a period of immunity to put on weight and regain peak condition. Some mixed fisheries may even open later than 1 April because their owners believe that this is too early for brown trout to have reached their optimum condition.

WINTER TROUT FISHING

When starting a winter campaign it is best to forget the niceties of trout fishing. Floating lines and nymphs are essentially summer techniques. Very occasionally, during unusually bright, mild weather, it may be possible to use nymphing tactics, but not very often. The best technique is to fish a sinking line and abandon flies and nymphs. Natural insects are sleeping out the winter and patrolling trout seek fish fry. Winter is the time for lures, particularly black and white fry imitations, such as Zonker, Appetiser, Viva and Dog Nobbler.

In winter, trout confine their feeding mostly to the deeper holes and troughs. Shallow water seldom produces fish. Skip the lure over the bottom. Competition for food is fierce among winter stocks so takes are normally savage, easily hookable affairs with the fish fighting hard.

Male rainbows are something of a rarity nowadays. Fishery owners stock their water mostly with triploid or female trout. For the angler this is good because the male trout tends to fight savagely and, when landed, is often in poor condition. The sterile triploid trout, on the other hand, retains its weight and appearance, making it a first-class sporting fish. Before paying to fish a water, therefore, it is advisable to ask about stocking policy and the type of fish being introduced. In this way you will avoid a bag of 'black' cock fish that are virtually inedible.

Spring Trout Fishing

Spring for the trout fisherman is from the first week in April until the end of May. With fine, warm springs increasingly something of the past, water temperatures seldom rise to any great extent during the first few weeks of the season and fly life is generally sparse. For this reason, stick to the sinking fly line throughout April.

Flies, however, may be varied a little. From late March nymphs, which have remained dormant throughout the winter, begin to stir, bringing a welcome change of diet to feeding trout whose attention is no longer confined to fry-imitating lures. Large lures will continue to catch fish, but for the angler wishing to use something resembling a natural insect, this is the time to make the change. Stick Fly, Montana Nymph in the black/green or black/red dressing, Invicta and Shrimp imitations all work well at this time of year.

The fast-sinking line can be discarded in favour of the slow-sinking line, enabling the angler to fish both the bottom and midwater layers. From the beginning of May floating lines are also worth trying. With a long leader and a weighted fly of the Nobbler type, the floating line can be used to inch the lure seductively back to the angler. Used with a nymph, these lines produce the most astounding takes and savage pulls, seen clearly on the floating line. This is exciting fishing and can produce some great results.

At this time of the season trout often pack together twenty-five to thirty yards (22.8–27.4m) offshore. Practise casting with a weight forward floating line and a 9–10 ft (3m) rod and you will often 'limit out' when other anglers fail to catch.

At the end of May waters which produce a mayfly hatch can provide fantastic sport and the trout become obsessed with these huge flies. Try using a Mayfly Nymph worked beneath the surface or, for greater excitement, a dry spent mayfly. To see a big trout delicately suck in a dry mayfly is one of the highlights of the trout anglers' year.

The trout (above and opposite).

THE GAME FISHING YEAR

A fine selection of trout flies.

SMALL RIVER FISHING

Not all trout fishing, of course, is done in put-and-take fisheries. Many clubs and associations have small river and even chalk stream fishing available to members. Spring on a small river is delightful and the fishing is often remarkably good. Small trout starved of food throughout the winter rise readily to a well-placed dry fly or tiny nymph.

For this type of fishing traditional flies are best – March Brown, Coch-y-Bondhu, Greenwell's Glory, to mention but a few. For nymph fishing, Copper Nymphs, Killer Bug, Shrimp or Pheasant Tail are all good catchers and well worth using. Heavy tackle of the type used on reservoirs or commercial fisheries is of little use on a stream. An 8ft 6 in (2.7 m) rod capable of throwing a No. 5 line is ideal. Your catch will mostly consist of small trout, but you can never tell when a big fish may appear to make your entire season.

SUMMER TROUT FISHING: JUNE to AUGUST

With the onset of summer, fishing for trout becomes increasingly difficult. The waters are rich in surface and subsurface insect life and the fish simply do not have to work for their food. It is at times and in conditions like these that the skilled dry fly

Trout fishing on the River Test.

and nymph fishermen come into their own. This is floating line time, when tiny Midge Pupa, Buzzers and minute dry flies score over the heavier lures.

As always, the weather plays a vital role. Humid days often produce a late afternoon or evening fly hatch that drive trout crazy. At these times long days on the lake or river are often wasted. Two hours at the right time will produce more fish than ten hours at the wrong time. The most productive times are late evening and early morning whether on lake, chalk stream or river. For the river angler, Iron Blue Dun, Sedge and Midge flies are likely to produce the best results. Nymphs such as the Leopard and Long Tailed Tit can also catch extremely well.

During the evening, when falling air temperatures and high water temperatures coincide, flies may hatch by the thousand. After waiting for this sort of hatch, trout will feed avidly and even huge brown and rainbow trout will start to rise. The sight of a 5 lb or 6 lb (2.7 kg) brown or double-figure rainbow sipping at hatching flies is enough to make even the most experienced angler tremble. When trout like this come firmly on feed, the dull days are forgotten. Oddly enough, it is not always easy to take a limit bag during these frantic feeding periods. The artificial fly may be superbly tied, but when it has to compete with the perfect, natural fly it is not always effective. A good tip at such times is to fish a nymph slightly subsurface. Fish which discriminate between hatching and free-flying insects often mop up a nymph without thought. Top nymphs are Damsel, Dever Springs and Pheasant Tail. Corixa can also fish well at this time of year and, for those anglers who prefer to fish lures, small Dog Nobblers and Richard Walker's Jersey Herd are well worth trying.

Interestingly, flies are subject to fashion. The Jersey Herd, for example, is a pattern which has rather fallen into obscurity in recent years, despite it being highly effective. The same is true of the Muddler and Whisky fly – both top catchers in their day but now rarely used. On a windy day, however, a Muddler fished on the surface is a summer fly hard to beat. Designed as a wake fly, the Muddler's deep hair head is built to throw water. Seen from below, it looks like a small crippled fish. Subsurface trout see it apparently struggling through the surface-film and lunge upwards to intercept it.

Summer trouting may not be easy, but it is exciting and, once mastered, can be highly productive.

AUTUMN TROUT

Like the curate's egg, autumn trout fishing is good in parts. The fish are obviously hungry, busily feeding in preparation for the cold winter to come. Such fish are often preoccupied with crane flies, otherwise known as 'Daddy Long Legs'. Crane fly hatch in bankside vegetation and are blown by autumn winds into the water. Millions of insects perish in this way and trout are quick to take advantage of this additional food source. Imitation crane fly, also called 'Daddy Long Legs', are deadly. Each fly is tied with carefully knotted legs to imitate the insect, and a good imitation is difficult to tell from the real thing. Highly competitive trout do not try. In a world where food is difficult to find, trout throw caution to the wind and stock up for the cold weather ahead. Once the crane fly season is over, switch to lures such as the Dog Nobbler or any other fry-imitating fly. These will keep fish coming until winter fishing starts or you decide to hang up your rods until the spring.

SALMON FISHING

Unless you are fortunate enough to live in an isolated area where salmon fishing is cheap, this branch of angling can cost a fortune. An increasing number of still water trout fisheries, however, are introducing salmon as a boost to sport and trade. These fish, weighing on average between 8 lb – 10 lb (3.6 – 4.5 kg) provide excellent sport on a fly rod. Most pre-stocked salmon fall to standard trout flies and lures, but are particularly attracted to dark flies.

Trevor Housby's Guide To Reservoir Trout Fishing

England

AVON
Blagdon, near Bristol (440 acres). Off A368 near junction with A38. Opens 31 March. Fly fishing only. One hour before sunrise to one hour after sunset. Boats 10a.m. to one hour after sunset. Run by Bristol Waterworks Co., Recreations Dept., Woodford Lodge, Chew Stoke, Bristol BS18 8XH. Tel: 0272 3323339.
Barrows Barrow Gurney (Barrow 1, 26 acres; 2, 39 acres; 3, 60 acres). Off A38, 5 miles (8 km) south of Bristol. Details as for Blagdon. Yearling stock only.
Chew (1200 acres). Details as for Blagdon. A Wessex Water Authority licence is required for fishing at Blagdon, Chew and Barrows.

BERKSHIRE
Queen Mother Reservoir, Datchet. Opens 13 March. Day ticket, evening, part-day, boat and bank. Tel: Roger Haynes 0753 684605.

CAMBRIDGESHIRE
Grafham Water near Huntingdon. (1600 acres). Stocked with browns and rainbows. Season for brown trout 2 April–31 October. Fishing one hour before sunrise to one hour after sunset. Run by Piscators (Grafham Water) Ltd. Tel: Jim Warren, 0480 810531.

CLEVELAND
Derwent Reservoir, Edmundbyers, near Consett (1000 acres). West of A68 junction with B6278. Stocked with browns and rainbows. Opens 1 May. Run by Sunderland and South Shields Water Co. Tel: 0207 55250.
Lockwood Beck Reservoir (40 acres). On A171 Guisborough to Whitby road. Limit eight fish. Run by Northumbrian Water Authority.
Scaling Dam Reservoir (120 acres). Also on A171 Guisborough to Whitby road. Opens 25 March. Run by Northumbrian Water Authority. Yorkshire Authority. Licence required. Limit eight fish.

CORNWALL
Argal Reservoir, Budock Penryn (65 acres). Season 1 April–31 October. Good dry fly water. Fishing one hour before sunrise to one hour before sunset. Fly only. Run by South West Water Authority (SWWA). Tel: Bob Evans 0326 72544.
Collisford Reservoir, Liskeard (900 acres). Off A30. Season 15 March–12 Oct. Brown trout only. Limit four fish over 10 in (25 cm). Self-service. Fly only. Run by SWWA. Tel: 0597 42366.
Crowdy Reservoir, Camelford (115 acres). Stocked with natural browns and rainbows as fry. Season 15 March–12 October. One hour before sunrise to one hour before sunset. Run by SWWA. Tel: 0579 42366.
Drift Reservoir, near Penzance (65 acres). Run by Trewidden estate. Tel: 0736 3869.
Siblyback Reservoir, St Cleer, Liskeard (140 acres). Details as Argal. Run by SWWA. Tel: Reg England 0579 42366.
Stithians Reservoir, near Helston (272 acres). Season 15 March–12 October. Limit four fish. All methods. Run by SWWA. Tel: 0326 72544.

CUMBRIA
Ghyll Head Reservoir, near Bowness (11 acres). Season 15 March–31 Dec. Day ticket. Fly only. Limit two fish. No wading. Run by Windermere Ambleside DAA. Tel: Martin Smith 09662 3750.

RESERVOIR TROUT FISHING

DERBYSHIRE
Foremark Reservoir, Milton, near Derby (230 acres). Four miles (6 km) east of Burton-on-Trent. Season 7 April–15 October. Run by Severn-Trent Water Authority. Tel: 0533 352011.
Linacre Reservoir, two miles (3 km) NW Chesterfield (26 acres). Season 1 April–30 September. Run by Severn-Trent Water Authority. Te.: J. G. Nixon 0246 473290. Yorkshire Water Authority licence required.
Ogston Reservoir, near Clay Cross (203 acres). Stocked with browns and rainbows. Opens 1 April. Limit two fish. Run by Derbyshire County Angling Club.

DEVON
Burrator Reservoir, Yelverton, Plymouth (150 acres). Run by South West Water Authority (SWWA). Tel: 06473 2440. Season 15 March–30 September. Contact Ray Timms, Burrator House, Burrator, Yelverton, or D.K. Sports, Vauxhall Street, Plymouth.
Fernworthy Reservoir, near Chagford (76 acres). Season 1 May–12 October. Tel: 06473 2440.
Gammaton, near Bideford (two lakes, 4 acres each). Season browns 1 April–30 September; rainbows 1 April–16 Dec. Run by Torridge Fly Fishing Club. Tel: S. Towers 023 72 77980. SWWA licence required.
Kennick & Tottisford Reservoir, Hennock, Bovey Tracey (45 and 35 acres). Season 1 April–31 Oct. Run by SWWA. Tel: 06473 2440.
Meldon Reservoir, near Okehampton (54 acres). Season natural brown 15 March–12 Oct. Run by SWWA.
Venford Reservoir, Holme, near Ashburton (33 acres). Season natural brown 15 March–12 Oct. Run by SWWA. Fishing free to holders of SWWA trout rod licence.

ESSEX
Ardleigh Reservoir, near Colchester (130 acres). Off A137 Harwich road. Season 26 March–30 Sept. Winter fishery fly only. Any legal method during Oct. Run by Ardleigh Reservoir Committee. Tel: 0206 230642.
Hanningfield Reservoir, near Chelmsford (600 acres). Opens 1 April. Bank 8a.m. to one hour after sunset. Run by Essex Water Co. Tel: 0268 710101.

KENT
Bewl Water, Lamberhurst (770 acres). Off A21 London to Hastings road. Season 3 April–30 October. Fly only. Sunrise to one hour after sunset. Run by Southern Water Authority. Tel: 0892 890661/890352.

LEICESTERSHIRE
Eye Brook Reservoir, Caldecott, near Market Harborough (400 acres). Opens 1 April. Fly only. One hour before sunrise to one hour after sunset. Run by Corby Water Co. Tel: 0536 770264.
Rutland Water, Whitwell, Oakham (3300 acres). Opens 1 April for browns and rainbows. Fly only. One hour before sunrise or 4.30a.m. to one hour after sunset. Run by Roger Thorn and Nick Dalby. Tel: 078 086 770.
Thornton Reservoir, near Leicester (75 acres). Opens 1 March (boats), 1 April (bank). Fly only. 8a.m. to half an hour after sunset. Run by Cambrian Fisheries. Tel: Ifor Jones 0530 230807.

LONDON
Barn Elms No.5 Reservoir, Merthyr Terrace, Barnes, SW13 (24 acres). Near Hammersmith Bridge. Season 12 March–30 November. Fly only. Run by Thames Water Authority. Tel: Chris King 01 748 3423.

NORTHAMPTONSHIRE
Pitsford Water, Pitsford (550 acres). Opens 1 April. Tel: 0604 781350.
Ravensthorpe Water, near Teeton, Northampton (100 acres). Open all year. Fly only. Tel: 0604 770875.

NORTHUMBERLAND
Bakethin & Kielder Water (140 and 2700 acres). Two linked waters between Kielder village and Bellingham. Seasons: Bakethin 1 May–30 Sept; brown trout, fly only. Kielder 1 March–31 Oct; browns and rainbows, fly and worm.

OXFORDSHIRE
Farmoor 11 Reservoir, Cumnor Road, Farmoor (240 acres). Open 28 March. Fly

Reservoir trout fishing.

only. 6.30a.m. to half an hour after sunset. Run by Thames Water Authority. Tel: The Warden 0865 863033.

SOMERSET
Clatworthy Reservoir, 15 miles (24 km) west of Taunton (130 acres). Season 26 March–11 Oct. Fly only. 8a.m. to one hour after sunset. Run by Wessex Water Authority (WAA). Tel: Dave Pursey 0984 23549.
Hawkridge Reservoir, 7 miles (11 km) west of Bridgwater (32 acres). Details as Clatsworthy. Run by WAA. Tel: 0278 424786.
Wimbleball Lake, Brompton Regis, Dulverton (374 acres). Season May 1–31 Oct. Fly only. Rainbows. One hour before sunrise to one hour after sunset. Run by SWWA. Tel: 039 87372.
Sutton Bingham Reservoir, 4 miles (6 km) south of Yeovil (142 acres). Season 22 March–11 Oct. Details as Clatsworthy. Run by WWA. Tel: 0935 872389.

STAFFORDSHIRE
Tittesworth Reservoir, The Lodge, Meerbrook, near Leek (139 acres). Season 31 March–15 Nov. Run by Tittesworth Fly Fishing Ltd. Tel: 053 834 389.

SUSSEX
Ardingly Reservoir, Ardingly, near Haywards Heath. Tel: 0444 892549 (in season).
Darwell & Powdermill Reservoirs, Mount-

field, near Robertsbridge (175 and 55 acres). Season 3 April–31 Oct. Fly only. Run by Hastings Flyfishers.
Weirwood Reservoir, Forest Row, East Sussex (280 acres). Rainbows. Opens 12 April. Tel: 034 282 2731.

WARWICKSHIRE
Draycote Water, Kites Hardwick, near Dunchurch, Rugby (600 acres). Opens 9 April. Run by Severn-Trent Water Authority. Tel: Mr Kerr (Kites Hardwick Filling Station) 0788 812018.
Shustoke Reservoir, near Coleshill (100 acres). Season 16 April–15 Oct. Fly only. Run by Shustoke Flyfishers. Tel: 0675 810702 or 021 743 4040.

YORKSHIRE & HUMBERSIDE
Embsay & Whinnygill Reservoirs (26 and 6 acres). Season 25 March–30 September. Fly, worm, minnow, spinning. 7a.m. to one hour after sunset. Run by Skipton AA. Tel: 0756 5435.
Damflask Reservoir, Low Bradfield, near Sheffield (115 acres). Off B6077. Season 25 March–30 Sept. Ticket machine on site. Any method but no livebaiting at various times. Run by YWA. Tel: 0742 26421 ext 2009.
Leighton Reservoir, Swinton Estate, Healey, near Marsham (105 acres). Opens 26 March. Fly only. Tel: 0765 89224.
Morehall Reservoir, Ewden Valley, near Sheffield (65 acres). Off A616. Opens 8 April. Fly only. Tel: 0742 26421 ext 2009.
Thornton Steward Reservoir, Bedale (34 acres). Opens 25 March. 8a.m. to one hour after sunset. No Sunday fishing. Fly only. Barbless hooks only. Run by YWA. Tel: 0677 50245.
Ulley Reservoir, near Rotherham (30 acres). Off B6067. Browns and rainbow. Details as Damflask.

WALES
CLWYD
Alwen Reservoirs (368 acres) on B4501 between Denbigh and Cerrig-y-Drudion. Season 30 March–17 Oct. Fly, worm, spinner. Contact: Vistors' Centre at Brenig Reservoir.
Dolwen and Plas Uchaf Reservoir (19 and 9 acres). Season 1 March–30 Sept. Tel: Llanefydd 244 or Rhuddlan 5900574.

DYFED
Llys y fran Reservoir, Maenclochog, near Haverfordwest (187 acres). Opens 18 March. Rainbow trout only. Run by WWA. Tel: 0437 4581 or Head Ranger on site, Tel: 09913 273.

GWENT
Llandegfedd Reservoir (430 acres). Season 20 March–17 October. Run by WWA. Tel: 049 5555122.

POWYS
Claerwen Reservoir (650 acres) near Rhayader. Fly only. Run by WWA. Tel: 0579 810449.
Clywedog Reservoir, near Llanidloes (612 acres). Opens 18 March. Run by Llanidloes AA. Tel: 05512 2644 after 7 p.m.

SOUTH WALES
Cantref Reservoir (42 acres). Off A470 Merthyr to Brecon road. Season 20 March–17 October. Extended season for rainbows.
Llanishen and Lisvane Reservoir, Cardiff (59 and 19 acres). Off B4562. Season 20 March–17 Oct. Fly only. Limit four fish.
Llwyn-on Reservoir (160 acres). On A470 at Cwm Taff Fishery. Season 20 March–17 Oct.
Tallybont Reservoir, 15 miles (24 km) south of Brecon (318 acres). Season 20 March–17 Oct. Tel: 087 487 237.
Usk Reservoir, 15 miles (24 km) west of Brecon (290 acres). Season 20 March–17 Oct. Self-service. Run by WWA. Tel: 0550 20422.

NATIONAL BODIES, CLUBS & ASSOCIATIONS

ENGLAND & WALES

Anglers' Co-operative Association
Director: Allen Edwards,
23 Castlegate,
Grantham,
Lincs NG31 6SW.
Tel: Grantham (0476) 61008.

Formed in 1948, the ACA is an anti-pollution organisation supported by anglers. It protects its members, now exceeding 10,000, by invoking the Common Law and fighting on members' behalf in the High Court. Over the years the ACA has lost only one case among the hundreds it has fought — and that was on a technicality.
Subscriptions
Life £50; annual £5; members of an ACA-affiliated club £3 p.a.; junior members (under 16) £1 p.a.

Angling Foundation
Prudential House,
10th Floor,
Wellesley Road,
Croydon CR0 9XY.
Tel: 01-681 1242.

The Angling Foundation was established in 1969 by the Angling Trade Association to promote and protect the present and future welfare of the sport of angling. The most significant undertaking to further the interests of the sport was the launch in 1986 of the 'Take a Friend Fishing' campaign, the largest such campaign in the history of the sport in the UK. The campaign is supported by the members of the Angling Trade Association, Water Authorities, tackle retailers, clubs and fishery owners. A second phase of the campaign, 'Fun Fish '88'', was launched in 1988, and backed by strong advertising, is aimed at children of all ages.

Companies wishing to join the Angling Trade Association should contact Ms Vanessa de Pemberton, Groups Manager, ATA, at the above address.

Angling Trade Association
Groups Manager: Vanessa de Pemberton.
Prudential House, 10th Floor, Wellesley Road, Croydon CR0 9XY.
Tel: 01-681 1242.
Formerly The British Association of Fishing Tackle Makers and Distributors, the ATA is a professional organisation run for the benefit of the British fishing tackle industry. It was set up to give manufacturers, wholesalers and distributors an opportunity to exchange views on any matter generally affecting the industry, to represent manufacturers, wholesalers and tackle dealers whenever the occasion may arise and to promote, develop and protect the interests of the fishing tackle trade. A requirement of membership is that the company must be a member of the British Sports and Allied Federation Ltd.

CLUBS & ASSOCIATIONS

Atlantic Salmon Trust
Director: Rear Admiral D. J. Mackenzie CB,
Moulin,
Pitlochry,
Perthshire PH16 5JQ.
Tel: Pitlochry (0796) 3439.

A charitable trust (patron HRH The Prince of Wales) which aims to conserve wild Atlantic salmon for the good of the community and to present the true facts concerning salmon. The Trust publishes Progress Reports twice a year which are sent out to subscribers. It also holds workshops and conferences from time to time.

Members subscribe to the Trust, preferably by Deed of Covenant.

British Carp Study Group
Secretary: Peter Mohan,
Heywood House,
Pill,
Bristol BS20 0AE.
Tel: Pill (027581) 2129.

An informal, non-political, independent social organisation, the BCSG was founded in 1969 by Peter Mohan and Eric Hodson. It was the world's first national organisation for carp anglers. Membership is open to all and there is no entrance qualification, although applicants must, in the opinion of the Committee, be experienced and successful carp anglers. The Group publishes *The Carp* magazine and to date has published four books. It also operates a free Carp Advisory Service which answers enquiries about carp from non-members.
Subscription for 1989
Annual £12, inc. £5 entry fee.

British Eel Anglers' Club
Secretary: Mick Bowles,
64 Granville Road,
Gillingham
Kent ME7 2PB.
Tel: Medway (0634) 54581.

Formed in 1980 by eel specimen hunters John Sidley, Gerry Rogers and Mick Bowles, the BEAC was a result of John Sidley's 'Put Eels Back Alive' campaign started in 1975. Members share a common interest in eel fishing and conservation. The Club offers advice to angling clubs and aims to prevent the netting of eels. *Eel News,* the club's magazine, is published four times a year. The Club also holds regular teach-ins and fish-ins in various parts of the country. Membership details may be obtained from:
John Sidley,
595 Reddings Lane,
Hall Green,
Birmingham B28 8TE.
Tel: Birmingham (021) 779802
Subscriptions
1 April 1988 – 31 March 1989.
Senior £8 (inc. £2 joining fee); junior (under 16) £4 (inc. £2 joining fee).

Carp Anglers' Association
Secretary: Peter Mohan,
Heywood House,
Pill,
Bristol BS20 0AE.
Tel: Pill (027581) 2129.

Although affiliated to the BCSG, the CAA, formed in 1975, is an independent organisation. Membership is more broadly based than the BCSG and members, currently numbering some 3000, are organised into twenty-five branches in England, Scotland, and abroad as far afield as the USA and Zimbabwe. Informally run, the Association has no rules or regulations and attracts carp anglers from beginners to the most experienced. A colour magazine, *The Carp Catcher,* is published three times a year.
Subscriptions
Annual £9 (inc. £1 joining fee).

Carp Society
Membership Secretary:
Vic Cranfield,
33 Covert Road,
Hainault,
Ilford,
Essex IG6 3AZ.

Formed in 1981 the aims of the Carp Society are: to entertain its members through its publications and meetings, to take some of the competitiveness out of carp fishing, to encourage carp men to adopt a moderate attitude in their fishing and to fish for pleasure rather than prestige, and to protect carp fishing and angling in general through a collective involvement in angling politics. The Society publishes a quarterly newsletter, *Cyrpinews*, and a magazine, *Carp Fisher*.
Subscriptions
New members' annual fee (1 Jan – 31 May 1989) £6.50 plus £1 joining fee. Full details from the Secretary.

Catfish Conservation Group
Membership Secretary:
John Deverell,
The Fishpool,
55 Gallows Hill,
Hertford,
Herts.

The Group was formed in 1984 to promote the conservation, understanding and stocking of catfish in English waters. A magazine, *Whiskers*, (edited by Kevin Maddocks) is published twice a year.
Subscriptions
£8 p.a. (inc. £2 joining fee).

Freshwater Biological Association
Director: Prof J. Gwynfryn Jones,
The Ferry House,
Far Sawrey,
Ambleside,
Cumbria LA22 0LP.
Tel: Windermere (096 62) 2468/9

The FBA has been researching the ecology and biology of freshwater organisms world-wide since 1929. It advises angling clubs on the practical management of reservoirs, lakes and rivers and the NAC is represented on its Council. Its Library is probably the finest in the world for freshwater biology. Membership is open to any who wish to support the Association. For details of membership contact Pamela Parry, Membership Secretary, at the above address.

Grayling Society
Secretary: Derek Froome,
3 Broom Road,
Hale,
Altrincham,
Cheshire WA15 9AR.

Inaugurated in 1977-78 to bring together those interested in the grayling and in grayling fishing. Since then the Society has done much to promote and publicise a proper appreciation of the grayling as a game fish among anglers, riparian owners, Water Authorities, conservationists, the sporting press and media generally. The Society also collects and records information on the distribution of the grayling throughout the UK and scientific and other data relating to its weight, growth rate, spawning, feeding, habitat and other information relevant to the species. An authoritative *Journal* is published twice yearly and is distributed to members together with a News Bulletin. Membership is open to anyone interested in the grayling and in grayling fishing.
Subscription
£5 p.a. (this includes the *Journal* and *Newsletter*).
Applications for membership may be made to the Membership Secretary, Mrs Claire Pickover, 20 Somersall Lane, Chesterfield, S40 3LA. Tel: 0246 568078.

National Anguilla Club
Secretary: Brian Crawford,
Water's Edge,
6 Holmer Lane,
Stirchley,
Telford,
Shropshire.
Tel: Telford (0952) 591131

The Club was formed in 1962 for eel angling specialists and is kept small to encourage close co-operation between members. Membership is open to experienced eel anglers who have achieved some success. Many of the country's leading anglers have been past members. The

Club is actively involved in angling politics for the preservation and conservation of eels and eel angling and works closely with NASA.
Subscription
£5 p.a.

National Anglers' Council
Executive Director:
P. H. Tombelson MBE,
11 Cowgate,
Peterborough PE1 1LZ.
Tel: Peterborough (0733) 54084.

The NAC was formed in 1966 to be the responsible body representing all anglers. Its membership includes the three major national angling bodies – the NFA, the NFSA and the Salmon & Trout Association – which, together with the Fishmongers' Company, make up the Foundation Members and part of the Executive Council. Association members include the ACS, the Angling Foundation, NASA and consultative organisations and angling clubs such as the London Anglers' Association and the Birmingham Anglers' Association.

The Council's objectives are to represent the sport of angling to the Government and the Sports Council on major issues and to co-ordinate grant aid to the sport. The NAC also runs the Sea Angling Liaison Committee of Great Britain and Ireland and the British Record (rod-caught) Fish Committee which produces the official list of British record fish.

The National Coaching Scheme and a Proficiency Awards Scheme which offers bronze, silver and gold awards in the three branches of the sport, is also run by the Council. Angling instructors are assessed and qualified by the Council which holds the National Register of Instructors.

Clubs which do not wish to become full voting members of the NAC may register for a place on the National Register of Clubs. The NAC is open to personal membership.

National Association of Specialist Anglers
General Secretary: Dr Bruno Broughton,
27 Ashworth Avenue,
Ruddington,
Nottingham NG11 6GD.
Tel: Nottingham (0602) 841703.

NASA began life in 1965 as the National Association of Specimen Groups and changed its name in 1982. The aims of NASA are to campaign for a healthy, unpolluted environment for fish and other forms of aquatic life, to protect fisheries and fish stocks, to promote comradeship and the interchange of information between anglers, and to encourage the young into angling, educating them to appreciate and respect fish and fisheries. Membership is open to all and is not restricted to big fish anglers. The Association publishes *Specialist Angler* magazine twice yearly and regular newsletters. NASA produces its own record fish list.
Subscriptions
£8.50 p.a. (Jan – Dec) plus £1 joining fee, juniors £5; affiliated membership:
Clubs & Associations under 100 members £1
100-200 members £20
Over 200 member..............£25
Further details about membership may be obtained from the Membership Secretary/Treasurer Neville and Kathy Fickling,
8 Kilgarth, 27 Lodge Lane,
Upton, Gainsborough, Lincs.
Tel: Gainsborough (0427) 83731.

National Federation of Anglers
Chief Administration Officer:
K. E. Watkins,
Halliday House,
2 Wilson Street,
Derby DE1 1PG.
Tel: Derby (0332) 36200.

Founded in 1903, the NFA is the biggest of Britain's angling organisations and the national organisation of coarse fishermen. The aims of the Federation are to promote measures for the improvement of the Freshwater Fisheries Laws, to fight against water pollution, to safeguard anglers' rights and privileges, to develop common fishing waters, and to deal with other matters concerning fisheries and angling in general. Membership is open to clubs and associations, not individuals. Any club wishing to join should apply to the CAO at the above address. The current club subscription rates start at £129 p.a. Newcomers to coarse fishing may find out through the NFA details about their local NFA-affiliated association or club.

NATIONAL FEDERATION OF SEA ANGLERS

National Federation of Sea Anglers
President/Secretary: R. W. Page
26 Downsview Crescent,
Uckfield,
Sussex TN22 1UB.
Tel: Uckfield (0825) 3589.

Founded in 1904, the NFSA formulates rules for sea angling which have become accepted as a pattern throughout the world. A founder member of the National Anglers' Council, the NFSA acts as watch-dog to protect the interests of sea anglers and is active in anti-pollution matters. In the interests of conservation it has laid down rules governing the minimum size at which species may be taken from boats and from shores or piers. Fish below these sizes must be returned to the sea.

With commercial sponsors the NFSA runs National Angling Championships and has encouraged junior membership by creating a National Junior Championship. One of the NFSA's most popular activities is its medals and awards competition for the capture of specimen sea fish. The competition is divided into two sections: section B for fish caught from boats and section S for fish caught from the shore, piers, harbour walls or break-waters.

As the foremost sea angling organisation in the country the NFSA deals with specific problems from member Clubs and individuals. Local divisions exist to deal with local problems and the needs of affiliated clubs.
Subscriptions
Personal membership
£5 p.a. plus £1 entrance fee.
Juniors (under 16) £2.50 plus £1 entrance fee.
Affiliation fees
Clubs with 10–25 members £25
Clubs with 26–50 members £30
Club with 51–100 members £40

An additional £10 is charged for every 50 members or part thereof thereafter, up to a maximum of £100.

Clubs seeking affiliation are required to pay a £2.10 entrance fee.

National Mullet Club
Secretary: David Rigden,
60 Powerscourt Road,
North End,
Portsmouth PO2 7JG.
Tel: Portsmouth (0705) 672330.

The Club aims to promote interest and efficiency in the sporting capture of the three British species of mullet and to promote their conservation. Membership is open to all. The Club publishes a bi-monthly magazine, organises fishing meetings, holds twelve annual trophy competitions, a 'Fish of the Month' competition and awards gold/silver/bronze certificates for notable catches. Advice and tuition is provided for beginners to the sport.
Subscriptions
£4 p.a. plus £1 optional joining fee for all competitions and certificate schemes.

Perchfishers
Secretary: Stewart Allum,
34 Markville Gardens,
Caterham,
Surrey CR3 6RJ
Opened to membership in 1987, the Perchfishers aim to promote and contribute to an understanding of perch and perch fishing. Membership is open to experienced perch anglers prepared to actively contribute to the aims of the club. A quarterly magazine is published and there are regular meetings and fish-ins held in various parts of the country. The club is currently producing *The Perchfisher's Book,* to be published in June 1990, and is also raising money for research into perch disease.
Subscriptions
£7 p.a. plus £1 joining fee.

CLUBS & ASSOCIATIONS

Shark Angling Club of Great Britain
Secretary & Treasurer:
Brian Tudor,
The Quay,
East Looe,
Cornwall PL13 1DX.
Tel: Looe (05036) 2642

The aims of the Club, affiliated to the International Game Fish Association, are to promote the sport of shark fishing, both nationally and world-wide, and to focus attention on the need to conserve sharks. To this end, the landing of underweight fish is discouraged. Members of the public, as well as Club members, may obtain information and assistance on any aspect of shark fishing at the Club's head office at Looe. Weighing facilities are also provided, as well as a social club for members. Membership is restricted to anglers who have caught, and had verified by a Weighmaster, a shark of 75 lb (34 kg) and over.
Subscriptions: £8.50 p.a. plus £2.50 joining fee.

The Light Tackle Club
21 Peacock Walk,
Bewbush,
Crawley,
West Sussex RH11 8DR.
Tel: Crawley (0293) 552396.

Formerly the British and European Line Class Angling Club (BELCAC), the Club adopted its new name, The Light Tackle Club (incorporating BELCAC), in March 1988. The objectives of the club are to promote the use of light tackle angling, to compile and keep up-to-date a list of British and European record fish in line classifications, to exchange data with other relevant bodies, to foster goodwill between anglers, to promote and encourage fish conservation and to assist in the protection of the marine environment.
Subscriptions:
Adult £5 p.a. plus £2 joining fee; junior/senior citizen £2.50. Full details of membership may be obtained from the Honorary Treasurer/Membership Registrar, D. Wood, 27 Beaver Close, Horsham, West Sussex RH12 4GB. Tel: Horsham (0403) 57075.

The Salmon and Trout Association
Director: James Ferguson, Fishmongers' Hall,
London Bridge,
London EC4R 9EL.

The Association was formed in 1903 to safeguard the salmon and trout fisheries of the United Kingdom. Today, individual membership is over 11,000, together with 150 clubs and associations representing 100,000 anglers. The Association campaigns for an end to drift netting in England and Wales and for more equitable migratory laws, to represent game fishers and their interests in Parliament and at a local level. It is also active against industrial and agricultural pollution and the increasing demands for water abstraction. Organised into forty-eight local branches, the Association provides angling and other facilities for members.
Subscriptions:
Full £12; husband/wife £16; junior (under 18 years) £6; family £24; life £250. Donations to the Association are most welcome.

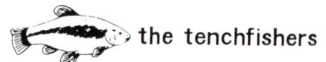

The Tenchfishers
Secretary: D. J. Reynolds,
Leppington,
Anchor Hill,
Knaphill,
Woking,
Surrey GU21 2HL.

Originally formed in 1954, the club was reformed in 1967 and now consists of anglers with a serious and sustained interest in tench fishing. The Tenchfishers aim to facilitate communication and the exchange of information and knowledge between members, to record tench catches by members, to undertake research into tench and tench fishing and, together with other angling bodies, to further the cause of tench fishing and angling generally. A *Bulletin* is published at regular intervals throughout the year.
Subscriptions
£8 p.a. plus £5 joining fee.

CLUBS & ASSOCIATIONS

Welsh Salmon and Trout Association
Honorary Secretary: M. J. Morgan,
Swyn Teifi,
Pontrhydendigaid,
Ystrad Meurig,
Dyfed.

Originally formed in 1947 as the Welsh Fly Fishing Association (the name was changed in 1978), the WSTAA is concerned with promoting excellence in angling, the encouragement of better angling facilities, the cultivation of friendship and sportsmanship among anglers, and to safeguard their interests. The Association has done much to encourage and coach young anglers and to provide facilities for disabled anglers. It has also been a leading campaigner against pollution and the encroachment of angling interests in Wales.
Subscriptions
Individual member £5 p.a.; clubs & associations £25 p.a.

Welsh Federation of Coarse Anglers,
6 Biddulph Rise,
Tupsley,
Hereford HR1 1RA.
Membership Secretary:
Mrs A. Mayers.

Formed in 1977, the Federation now has a membership of over fifty affiliated clubs representing some 12,000–15,000 individual Welsh anglers. The aims of the Federation are to obtain as full a representation as possible of Welsh coarse anglers; to improve, in association with the Welsh Water Authority, existing fisheries and increase the availability of coarse fishing waters; to remove present restrictions on coarse fishing in Wales; to obtain representation on *all* Fisheries Committees; to advise on legislation affecting coarse angling and to co-operate to the fullest extent with all other water users. Apart from international competitions, the Federation organises the Welsh National Championships and participates in the Champion of Champions competition. Junior competitions are also arranged to encourge more young anglers into the sport. A coaching scheme is available to members offering expert tuition. Membership is open to all Welshmen, including 'exiled' Welsh anglers.
Subcriptions
£10 p.a. per angling club.

SCOTLAND

Angler's Co-operative Association (Scotland)
Secretary: Malcolm W. Thomson,
21 Heriot Row,
Edinburgh EH3 6EN.
Tel: 031-225 6511.

The ACA Scotland (patron HRH The Duke of Edinburgh) was established in 1948 for the prime purpose of fighting polluters of water, to secure reparation for fish kills caused by pollution and for restocking waters when returned to a pure state. The ACA works closely with the River Purification Boards of Scotland who present cases of pollution for prosecution in the criminal courts. The ACA then proceeds to take the polluters to the civil courts.

The ACA is a voluntary organisation run by anglers for the angling community at large and relies on members' subscriptions and an annual prize draw for its income.
Subscription
Life membership..................£20
Annual members....................£2
Members of affiliated Clubs
....£1
Clubs, Associations and Federations: £4 per 50 members up to a maximum of £40.
Hotel, trade members and estates: minimum £5.

Law And The Angler
by Michael Gregory, LL.B.

The law can be a good friend to the angler, so long as she or he keeps within it. This article aims to show anglers how not to fall foul of some of the basic laws and to indicate the strength of the law as an ally to the angler. For simplicity the angler is referred to as male, but as in law, any masculine reference includes both sexes.

Fishing Rights
Strong Legal Protection

Fishing rights are property. From this simple statement stems the strong protection the law gives to the owners and occupiers of fisheries or fishing rights, whether they are owned outright or held under a tenancy. Legal remedies are available, and readily given by the courts, against interference with fisheries and the enjoyment of anglers, be it by trespass, pollution, unlawful abstraction, legal obstruction of the passage of migratory fish or whatever. If proceedings have to be taken the court can order the payment of damages and, where appropriate, make an injunction (that is, an order to stop it). Failure to comply with a court injunction is serious. It is a contempt of court for which the malefactor may be sent to prison.

My advice to clubs or others wishing to obtain fishing rights is to purchase them if they can. If not, try to get a tenancy, long, short or from year to year. If the owner is wary of granting a tenancy more than, say, a year, he might be persuaded that more care and resources would be devoted to fishery management the longer the security of tenure.

Powers of Bailiffs

Officially appointed bailiffs have wider powers than private bailiffs. They are treated as constables for enforcing statutory fishing laws. They may examine fishing tackle, search boats, 'seize any fish and any instrument, vessel, vehicle or other thing' being used by poachers, and arrest poachers.

Private bailiffs (e.g. club bailiffs) can only act on the property of their employers and within their authority. They can turn off trespassers, may arrest night poachers without a warrant, and also day poachers found using illegal fishing methods. 'Any person' may seize for production in court the tackle or anything else a poacher has with him for taking or destroying fish. The court can order it to be forefeited. Any rod licence holder can require someone found fishing to produce his licence and to state his name and address. Bailiffs should always carry their written authority.

Permissions and Licences

Before fishing the angler needs the right to fish. Except for the high seas, all waters and land are owned by somebody. Most tidal waters are owned by the Crown, and there are public fishing rights in them. There are no public fishing rights in non-tidal waters, and so the angler, if not the owner, requires permission to fish – e.g. by joining a club that owns or leases the fishery, or by purchasing a day or season ticket (if available), or by obtaining the owner's consent.

Getting the right to fish is not the end of the story. It is illegal to fish in England and Wales (except in the sea) without a Water Authority licence (a rod licence), though some fisheries (not many) get a general licence to cover everyone who fishes. Note that a rod licence is not a permission to fish: the owner's permission is also needed.

Some Prohibitions

Byelaws.

Byelaws made by official bodies have the force of an Act of Parliament. Water Authorities have Fishery Byelaws, which are a list of do's and don'ts. It is a punishable offence to contravene them. They usually include, among other things, size limits for each species of fish, bag limits, rules about the number of rods and hooks an angler may use, and about keep nets. They also specify the price of rod licences and set out close seasons.

Close Seasons

It is a punishable offence to fish for, take, kill or attempt to take or kill a fish during its close season or weekly close time. There is no close season for sea fish. The close seasons for rod and line fishing are specified by each Water Authority in byelaws. The standard close seasons are set out elsewhere in this book.

Illegal Fishing Methods

An Act of 1975 forbids the use of certain fish-taking devices and methods familiar to poachers – including firearms, sundry instruments for foul-hooking fish, spears, snares, set lines, explosives, poisons, electrical devices, lights and fish roe as bait. Unbarbed gaffs and tailers may be used 'as auxiliary to angling with the rod and line'. Byelaws may add to the list in particular localities. It is also an offence to have possession of prohibited instruments with the intention of using them to take or kill fish.

Immature and Spawning Fish

It is an offence to knowingly (or attempt to) take, kill or injure unclean or immature fish. If an angler, however, takes the fish accidentally and returns it to the water with the least possible injury, no offence has been committed.

Another offence is wilfully to disturb any spawn or spawning fish, or any bed, bank or shallow in which spawn or spawning fish may be.

Lead Weights

Regulations prohibit the supply of 'lead weights for the purpose of weighting fishing lines', if the weights are over 0.06 grams and under 28.35 grams. Importation of lead for this purpose is also illegal. Lead-cored fishing lines, and swim-feeders, self-cocking floats and flies incorporating lead are not prohibited. Although the Regulations do not prohibit the use of the weights, it is illegal to supply, most Water Authorities have recently done so by byelaws. Thames Water Authority obtained a conviction in April 1988 of an angler using lead shot. He was fined £50 with £47 costs.

Rating

Fishing rights are rateable, but only if they are severed from the occupation of the land. A grant of a fishing lease or licence does not sever them unless the grant is by deed under seal. Where an angling club holds rateable fisheries or premises it can apply to the local authority for discretionary relief against some or all of the rates.

Privatisation

The Government intends within the next year to privatise the Water Authorities. This will be a golden opportunity to improve our rivers and fisheries at last because the intention is to extend the present statutory duty 'to maintain, improve and develop' fisheries and transfer the duty to a National Rivers' Authority. This new Authority will be responsible for the wholesomeness of rivers and pollution control. It will be important to get the structure right so that the Regional Fishery Advisory Committees will continue to be effective.

The Freshwater and Saltwater Fishes of the British Isles
by Len Cacutt

Coarse Fishing

The fishes found in Britain's freshwaters were present from the time when the North Sea and English Channel were formed at the end of the last Ice Age, about 10,000 years ago. There are a number of other species which are found on the continent of Europe, but these had not found their way into Britain's waters by that time. We call the naturally found fishes in British waters 'indigenous' to this country.

Barbel
Found only in, gravelly, strong-flowing water where it feeds head-down, the barbel is a stubborn fighter when hooked. It is confined to central and southern England and has been introduced into suitable waters by anglers. The record barbel catch, caught from the Hampshire Avon, weighed 13 lb 12 oz (6.237 kg).

Bream
The common or bronzed bream and the much rarer silver bream live in waters of the East Coast. Both are deep-bodied, browsing, herbivorous fishes, the common bream reaching quite large weights, with a record from Staffordshire standing at 16 lb 6 oz (7.427 kg). The silver bream does not appear on the British Record (Rod-caught) Fish list and awaits a minimum catch of 1 lb (0.454 kg).

Carp
While the roach, bream, dace, chub, tench, gudgeon, bleak, minnow, rudd, and even the goldfish, are members of the carp family, all identifiable from comparisons of the pharyngeal (throat) teeth, the true common carp is easily the largest. Slow-flowing, lowland rivers and enclosed waters will all support this charismatic fish and its varieties, the king, mirror and leather, but none of these is recognised as a separate species. The heaviest carp taken in British waters is a 53 lb 6 oz (24.0 kg) common carp caught in 1986. Other close relatives are the grass carp, a comparatively new introduction to Britain, which reaches 16 lb (7.257 kg), and the crucian carp, a much smaller, but very attractive, golden-brown fish, the record for which is 5 lb 10 oz 8 dr (2.565 kg).

Catfish
An introduced species and a particularly ugly one, the catfish, properly called the wels, can grow to enormous sizes, up to 440 lb (300 kg), on the continent, where it is widespread. In Britain it is known so far up to 70 lb (32 kg). It is found in a few lakes in Britain near Woburn Abbey, where it was first introduced, and has probably reached one or two nearby rivers.

Chub
The predatory member of Britain's carp-related group of fishes, the chub shares the same kind of flowing water as the barbel, growing to at least 8 lb (3.6 kg), with the British record at 7 lb 6 oz (3.345 kg). A record chub of 10 lb 8 oz (4.7 kg) once sat at the head of the British Record list but was removed as not being proven. The chub feeds on insects and larvae when young but adult chub take small fish and even suitably sized terrestrial animals that have fallen in can be swallowed.

Dace
The fast-swimming dace in the British Record Fish list weighed 1 lb 4½ oz

(0.574 kg), so it does not reach the size of chub, the fish with which it is most confused. A comparison between the anal and dorsal fins, however, soon identifies them. The dace lives in sparkling, fast-running water and feeds on small insect life below and on the surface, where it can be caught on small artificial flies.

Eel
There are few rivers or enclosed waters that do not hold eels, although large speciments of 10 lb and over are rare. Most anglers try to avoid catching the wriggling, slippery eel, but there is a thriving eel specimen group. The record eel weighed 11 lb 12 oz (5.046 kg).

Grayling
This handsome fish has an adipose fin, the sign that it is related to the salmon and trout family, although it is found in the same habitat as chub and dace. The grayling is considered to be at least as good eating as trout. The biggest British grayling weighed 3 lb 10 oz (1.644 kg).

Orfe, Golden
Yet another cyprinid and related to the chub, the orfe is found in the British Isles although it is not a native fish. An ornamental variety, the golden orfe, has a record weight of 4 lb 12 oz (2.154 kg). This goldfish-like species probably escaped from an ornamental pond and found suitable breeding conditions.

Perch
For many anglers, the perch is the most attractive of all British freshwater fishes, with its dark, vertical bars and bright red fins and spiny dorsal fin, held erect as it surges into a shoal of fry in search of food. It is widespread throughout Britain in rivers and enclosed waters and is a favourite with young anglers due to its liking for all kinds of hookbait.

Pike
The largest and most fearsome of British freshwater predators, the pike can reach weights up to and beyond 40 lb (18 kg), but any fish over 10 lb (4.5 kg) is likely to be female. Sadly, game fishery owners and bailiffs tend to remove all pike from their waters in the mistaken belief that their trout are threatened. The British Record (rod-caught) pike weighed 42 lb (19.05 kg). It appears that a pike can eat a prey half its own weight, although this is, of course, not common.

Roach
The most sought-after species in the coarse anglers' preferred list, the roach is widespread throughout Britain's lowland rivers and enclosed freshwaters. The adult is a handsome, red-eyed and red-finned fish, but can, unless controlled, colonise a water with large shoals of adult but stunted specimens. The British Record (Rod-caught) is 4 lb 10 oz (1.842 kg).

Rudd
This coarse fish's deep body with its attractive golden tint makes the rudd distinguishable from the roach. Its feeding habits are also different from other similar species with the exception of the dace, and because the rudd takes floating food from the surface it can be caught by fly fishing methods. The rod-caught record weighed 4 lb 10 oz (2.097 kg).

Tench
The body slime of this very handsome, easily recognisable, tan-gold bodied cyprinid was once thought to have curative properties for injured fish and was named the Doctor Fish. The tench lives in the depths of quiet, muddy waters where it feeds on small aquatic insects and plant life. It grows large, the current rod-caught record weighing 12 lb 8 oz 11 dr (5.689 kg).

Pike-Perch (Zander)
The proper name for this predator is Zander, which avoids any possibility of it being thought of a cross between the pike and the perch, which it certainly is not. It occurs naturally in continental Europe and is not native to British waters, having been introduced into lakes in England in the 1870s, from where it has spready widely in East Anglian rivers,

fens and drains. Not as large as the pike, the zander has a record weight of 17 lb 4 oz (7.824 kg). A related species, the walleye, is also found in the British Record (rod-caught) list at 11 lb 12 oz (5.329 kg), but it is the only specimen ever recorded and must be considered either as a mis-identification or a single specimen that somehow found its way into the River Welney, Norfolk, where it was captured in 1934.

Bleak, Gudgeon, Minnow
These three small cyprinids are often little more than a nuisance. They are often caught by anglers either by accident, for live-baits or the bleak by matchmen to build up a total weight. They teem in many British rivers and still waters and will compete with more 'respectable' fish such as roach and bream for the angler's hooked bait. Record weights are listed: bleak and gudgeon, 4 oz 4 dr (0.120 kg); minnow, 13 dr (0.023 kg).

Ruffe
This little spiny fish might be mistaken for a small perch or zander, but reference to the dorsal fins soon identifies it. It is found in slow-moving water as far north as Loch Lomond but reported as rare in Wales. It is the largest of the small nuisance fishes, with a record weight of 5 oz 4 dr (0.148 kg), and although it is reported to be tasty, it is too small to be valuable.

Bullhead
Another small fish avoided by anglers, the bullhead has a spined dorsal fin and is found under stones in English and Welsh rivers and streams. It is only taken by accident by anglers fishing with maggot or worm on fine tackle. The record is 1 oz (0.023kg)

Pumpkinseed
This small sunfish is a visitor from South America, where it reaches weights up to 1 lb 6 oz (0.63 kg), but it has established itself in a few sheltered waters in England and the heaviest so far weighed 2 oz 10 dr (0.074 kg). There is a possibility that some caught by anglers are the result of pet fish being released into local waters.

Whitefishes
This group of small silver fishes, all belonging to the *Coregonus* species, are the result of the last Ice Age and were migratory fishes before being cut off as the retreating ice formed deepwater lakes. The schelly (skelly), or gwyniad, is confined to Lake Bala in Wales, and two enclosed waters in the Lake District, and has a record weight of 1 lb 10 oz (0.737 kg) The pollan and vendace may be the same species and live in Irish loughs and the Lake District, while the powan, which is closely related to the schelly, is found only in Loch Lomond and Loch Eck. The pollan, vendace and powan have no British rod-caught record weights listed.

GAME SPECIES

Salmon
The salmon is acclaimed as the king of fishes, and is the fish most sought by wealthy freshwater anglers. In British rivers the Atlantic salmon reigns, and although its numbers have severely diminished due to industrial pollution, it appears each year in sufficient numbers to attract a large number of keen anglers. There have been serious attempts to revive a run of salmon up the Thames, and by 1976 four dead specimens in various states had been identified in the river. Then in September 1983 an angler caught a 6 lb 12 oz (3.06 kg) salmon at Chertsey, some 150 years after the last recorded fish. The British Record (rod-caught) salmon is an old one, at 64 lb (29.029 kg), dating back to 1922. Strangely, a wayward coho salmon appears in the British record book, a fish of 1 lb 8 oz 1 dr (0.681 kg) caught off Guernsey, Channel Isles. It was perhaps a stray from fish farming attempts in Scotland.

Trout
The native brown trout and its migratory form, the sea trout, are widespread throughout Britain in rivers and enclosed waters, some of which are stocked by fish-farm bred specimens. Reservoir fishing for the brown trout and the introduced rainbow trout is very big business

countrywide and has been the means of introducing thousands of ertswhile coarse anglers to the pleasures of fly fishing. The rainbow has been induced to breed naturally in very few waters. Another introduced fish, the American brook trout, is in fact a charr and has established itself in but a few waters in Scotland, the West Country and Sussex. The British Record (rod-caught) brown trout weighed 19 lb 9 oz 4 dr (8.880 kg); the rainbow 21 lb 4 oz 4 dr (9.645 kg), the sea trout 20 lb (9.071 kg), and the American brook trout 5 lb 13 oz 8 dr (2.650 kg).

Charr

This fish is better described as the arctic charr to differentiate it from the American brook trout, also a charr. The arctic charr is a migratory fish not often caught in Britain, but a rodcaught record of 3 lb 4 oz (1.480 kg) indicates that it does reach these waters. There are, or were, various land-locked populations of charr and like the whitefishes were the result of the formation of deepwater lakes when the ice-caps retreated some 10,000 years ago. It was thought that about 200 lochs, loughs and lakes once held charr, many of which were given different scientific descriptions until it was understood that they were all basically the same species but had evolved different characteristics due to their isolation.

SEA SPECIES

The seas round Britain are host to a vast number of fish species, never seen or known by the angler. Even the inshore regions hold sea fishes unknown to any but the marine biologist, and the deeps, of course, are occupied by many rare and often quite grotesque kinds. Most of the fishes which are familiar on the fishmonger's slab can be caught by the sea angler, but some, such as the haddock, are more often netted by trawlers. The angler's sea species introduced below are those most often taken by sportfishermen. The British Record (rod-caught) list for sea fishes has separate records for boat and shore, as well as a list of 'mini' records, fish up to 1 lb (0.453 kg). Here, only the heaviest weight of each species is given.

Spurdog, Smooth Hound and Starry Smooth Hound

All these fish are species of dogfish which are very similar in shape and size and which are found in similar locations around the coast, although the Smooth Hounds prefer silty ground. The spurdog may grow up to about 20 lb (9 kg) and is also netted commercially as 'rock salmon'. Both the Smooth Hound and the Starry Smooth Hound curiously share the same rod-caught record weight of 28 lb (12.7 kg), although the two fish were taken at entirely different places.

Lesser Spotted Dogfish

This is smaller than the bullhuss, the other common British dogfish, many sea angling festivals being won by large weights of this unfortunate species. The rod-caught record for the lesser spotted is 4 lb 1 oz 13 dr (1.865 kg). Both this and the bullhuss are identified by their complex nasal flap formation. For non-sea anglers, fried fish-shops call this very tasty food 'rock salmon'.

Black-Mouth Dogfish

So far as the angler is concerned, this is a much rarer dogfish since it is not often met in water shallower than thirty fathoms, and usually stays at depths up to 200 fathoms, although there is a record weight of 2 lb 13 oz 8 dr (1.288 kg). One distinguishing feature is a longer lobe to the tailfin.

Sole

Although the colour of these flatfish varies, they are all oval in shape with the mouth right at the tip of the head. Most soles are dark brown in colour with a few much darker patches. They feed mainly at night and specimens weighing about 5½ lb have been caught on occasion.

Common Skate

Anglers differentiate between the skates and rays more or less by their size, the skates being considerably larger. A very formidable fish for the angler, because of its sheer bulk, the current rod-caught record standing at 227 lb (102.961 kg). Extremely powerful and stout tackle is needed to boat such a fish, its 'wings' creating a suction on the seabed as well as acting on the currents, making playing monster skate a muscle-straining business. It is found all round the British Isles, but anglers fish for them off the Hebrides and Orkneys.

Bass
One of the great game sea fishes, the spiny and silvery bass provides sport from both boat and shore practically all round the coast. When small, bass tend to keep in shoals, but the big double-figure specimens sought by the angler are usually solitary fish living near reefs where plenty of small fish provide food. Britain's largest bass came from the Kent coast and weighed 19 lb 9 oz 2 dr (12.757 kg).

Bream, Black
The story of the decline in numbers of this handsome fish makes sad reading. Once prolific off the Sussex coast, where it came to breed, the black bream attracted vast numbers of anglers who amassed huge catches during regular bream festivals. But the death of a single specimen filled with roe means the death of hundreds, of bream and these depredations so reduced the numbers of black bream off that area of the coast that fewer and fewer were being caught. The fish is still found in many areas off the south coast, where off Cornwall the current record of 6 lb 14 oz 4 dr (3.125 kg) was taken.

Cod
This is possibly the most sought-after fish for two reasons; one is that it reaches weights well over 50 lb (22.6 kg), and the other is its culinary value. When gaping open while being played to the surface, the extremely large mouth of the cod acts as a brake and puts considerable pressure on terminal tackle and rod. the heaviest cod caught from British waters weighed 53 lb (24.038 kg), and the shore record is a very commendable 44 lb 8 oz (20.183 kg) caught by a young anler who thought he was pulling ashore a mass of weed.

Haddock
Closely related to the cod, the haddock is mostly taken from boats in northern waters, and can reach more than 10 lb (4.5kg) in weight. It has three dorsal fins and two anal fins, with a brownish-black shading and a silvery belly. A dark spot, known as a thumbprint, is situated just above the pectoral fin.

Ling
The ling is a member of the cod family which can reach over 6 ft (1.8m) in length and over 50 lb (22 kg) in weight. The largest catches are generally taken from wrecks where the ling lives like the conger, hunting live food from the deep waters.

Flounder
This flattie seems not to know whether it is a salt or a freshwater fish. It has been known to travel miles upstream from the sea and has even been caught in freshwater, but at sea it is found down to depths of at least 160 ft (50 m). As might be suspected from its habits, the boat and shore records are close, that from boats being 5 lb 11 oz 8 dr (2.593 kg) and from shore 5 lb 2 oz (2.324 kg).

Halibut
Easily the largest flatfish in British waters and once called the last of the gamefish, this huge flattie can reach weights of over 600 lb (272 kg). The halibut is not found in the English Channel, anglers having to travel north to do battle with the monster, but to beat the record some very strong angler will have to haul over the gunwales a fish over 234 lb (106.136 kg), the existing top weight.

Mackerel
Most sea anglers think of this very oily, tasty fish as the best bait for all other species and use teams of six coloured feathers to lure them, but the mackerel is a relative of the tunnys and other powerful big game fish, so on its own

account can provide excellent sport on light, single-hook tackle. Most school mackerel weigh about a pound but the record stands at a remarkable 6 lb 2 oz 7 dr (2.790 kg), a weight once thought totally impossible for the species.

Garfish

The garfish is a relative of the flying fish, with a long beak-like jaw and many small, sharp teeth. Its colouration is similar to that of the mackerel and it is a small fish, rarely weighing more than 2 lb (1 kg). If it is hooked, it is usually an indication that big mackerel are not too far away.

Pollack

One of the great sporting members of the cod family, the record pollack grew to a handsome 29 lb 4 oz (13.267 kg). This is a predatory fish that hovers above and round steep-sided rocky reefs and feeds on small shoalfish. Anglers find exciting sport with pollack by using pirks and lures while drifting over wrecks.

Coalfish

On the other side of the Atlantic (where they call it the 'pollack' just to confuse things) the coalfish reaches very considerable weights of over 40 lb (18 kg), but for some reason British waters have not so far yielded one that heavy, the record standing at 37 lb 5 oz 616.923 kg). It is taken over the same kind of marks where pollack are caught but does not provide quite the same stirring fight on rod and line.

Rays

The skates (see Common Skate) and rays are a group of soft-boned, flattened round fish with no relationship to the plaice, turbot, flounder and so on. With a record weight of 96 lb 1 oz (43.571 kg), the electric ray is the heaviest of the group on the British Record list, with the marbled electric ray the smallest at 2 lb 8 oz 8 dr (1.148 kg). Some, such as the small-eyed, or painted ray (16lb 6 oz 8 dr (7.441 kg) and the undulate ray (21 lb 4 oz 8 dr (9.652 kg)), have very localised distributions, while the thornback, the most common, is found all round the British Isles. Its record weight stands at 38 lb (17.236 kg).

Whiting

While the angler is winter fishing for his favourite cod it is very likely that he will sooner or later find himself winding-in a whiting or two, for shoals of this much smaller cod-relative often join forces with cod on the move round the Kent coast from the North Sea. Some anglers, recognising the jerky bites of a whiting will leave the hooked fish down there in the hope that it will be engulfed in the cavernous mouth of a large cod. No great shakes in size, the record British whiting weighs 6 lb 12 oz (3.061 kg).

Turbot

This large flattie's attraction for anglers is two-fold: it grows to a good size, with a record weight of 33 lb 12 oz (15.308 kg), and it joins the bass as one of the most welcome and delicious fishes that any angler can take home with him after a day at sea. The best ones come from shallow shell-grit banks off the south-west coast, such as the famous Skerries, with a few coming from marks farther east. A close relative of the turbot is the smaller brill, the record for which is 16 lb (7.257 kg), caught from the same kind of mark.

Mullet

There are three species of grey mullet in British waters, the golden grey, the thick-lipped and the thin-lipped, all of which are incredibly shy and difficult to induce to take a hooked bait. All are found predominantly in the brackish water of estuaries or harbours but, when really cold weather sets in, they seem to move out to deep water. Largest is the thick-lipped with a record weight of 10 lb 1 oz (4.564 kg), the thin-lipped weighed 3 lb 7 oz (1.599 kg) and the golden grey 1 lb 14 oz 4 dr (0.857 kg). The red mullet, seen frequently on wet-fish slabs, belongs to a different, tropical genus and has a record weight of 3 lb 7 oz (1.559 kg).

FISH SPECIES

Wrasse
Largest of the wrasse group of rock-haunting fishes is the ballan with a record weight of 9 lb 6 oz (4.252 kg) and the area to fish for them are the seas off the west coast. The smallest wrasse is the Baillon's wrasse, found in the list of min-records at a monumental 1 oz 7 dr (40 g). Other members of this colourful and attractive group are the rock cook, scale-rayed, goldsinny, corkwing, lesser and cuckoo and all should be returned immediately after capture.

Plaice
Nearly as sought-after as the turbot, the plaice is another flattie with a great eating reputation. Commercial trawling means the exposed sandbanks have been scoured clean of plaice and other edible fish, but the tasty flattie can still be found in estuaries and on rough-ground marks. The record plaice is a respectable 10 lb 3 oz 8 dr (4.635 kg) and even the shore top weight stands at 8 lb 2 oz 12 dr (3.706 kg).

Sharks
British waters have a big reputation for large sharks, with the world record porbeagle of 465 lb (210.910 kg) coming from a mark off Cornwall. The mako record is also respectable at 500 lb (226.786 kg), caught over the famous Eddystone Reef. Most popular is the blue, but its numbers and average size are declining due to over-fishing and the disgraceful habit of killing even the smallest blues instead of releasing them to put on weight and, more important, help to conserve the species. The thresher, with its unmistakable and extraordinary long upper lobe to the tail fin, the same length as the rest of the body, has a record weight of 323 lb (146.504 kg). One other shark, comparatively rare in British waters, is the six-gilled, which can reach considerable weights in warmer waters, but in the British Record list is a mere 9 lb 8 oz (4.309 kg).

Monkfish
Despite its somewhat grotesque appearance, the monkfish is a member of the shark family which is highly prized for its culinary value. It is a big fish which can weigh more than 70 lb (32 kg) and it generally gives anglers a good fight before being safely landed! The monkfish is sandy-brown on the back with several blotchy marks which create perfect camouflage.

Tope
This fish is called a small shark, but anyone who hooks a tope of 50 lb (22.5 kg) or over will wonder at this description, for the tope can put up a remarkable struggle as it circles on the surface round the boat and refuses to be drawn to the net or gaff. The Essex coast, unusually, provided the record tope, which stands at a very fine 79 lb 12 oz (36.172 kg).

Gurnards
There are four gurnards on the British Record list, the largest, the tub or yellow, weighing 11 lb 7 oz 4 dr (5.195 kg). The other three are the grey (2 lb 7 oz (1.105 kg)), the red (5 lb (2.268 kg)) and the streaked (1 lb 6 oz 8 dr (0.637 kg)). All these fish have strange, square, armoured heads, and spined fins and are widely distributed round our coasts.

THE FISHERMAN'S YEARBOOK **COARSE FISH** 65

Barbel

Chub

Bream

COARSE FISH

Wild Carp

Dace

Crucian Carp

COARSE FISH

Roach

Perch

Eel

COARSE FISH

Zander

Bleak

Grayling

THE FISHERMAN'S YEARBOOK   **COARSE FISH**   **69**

Gudgeon

Tench

Rudd

Ruffe

COARSE FISH

Wels Catfish

Pike

GAME FISH — 71

Charr

Sea Trout

Salmon

GAME FISH

Brown Trout

Rainbow Trout

Brook Trout

THE FISHERMAN'S YEARBOOK — SEA FISH — 73

Bass

Mullet

Pollack

SEA FISH

Haddock

Whiting

Cod

SEA FISH

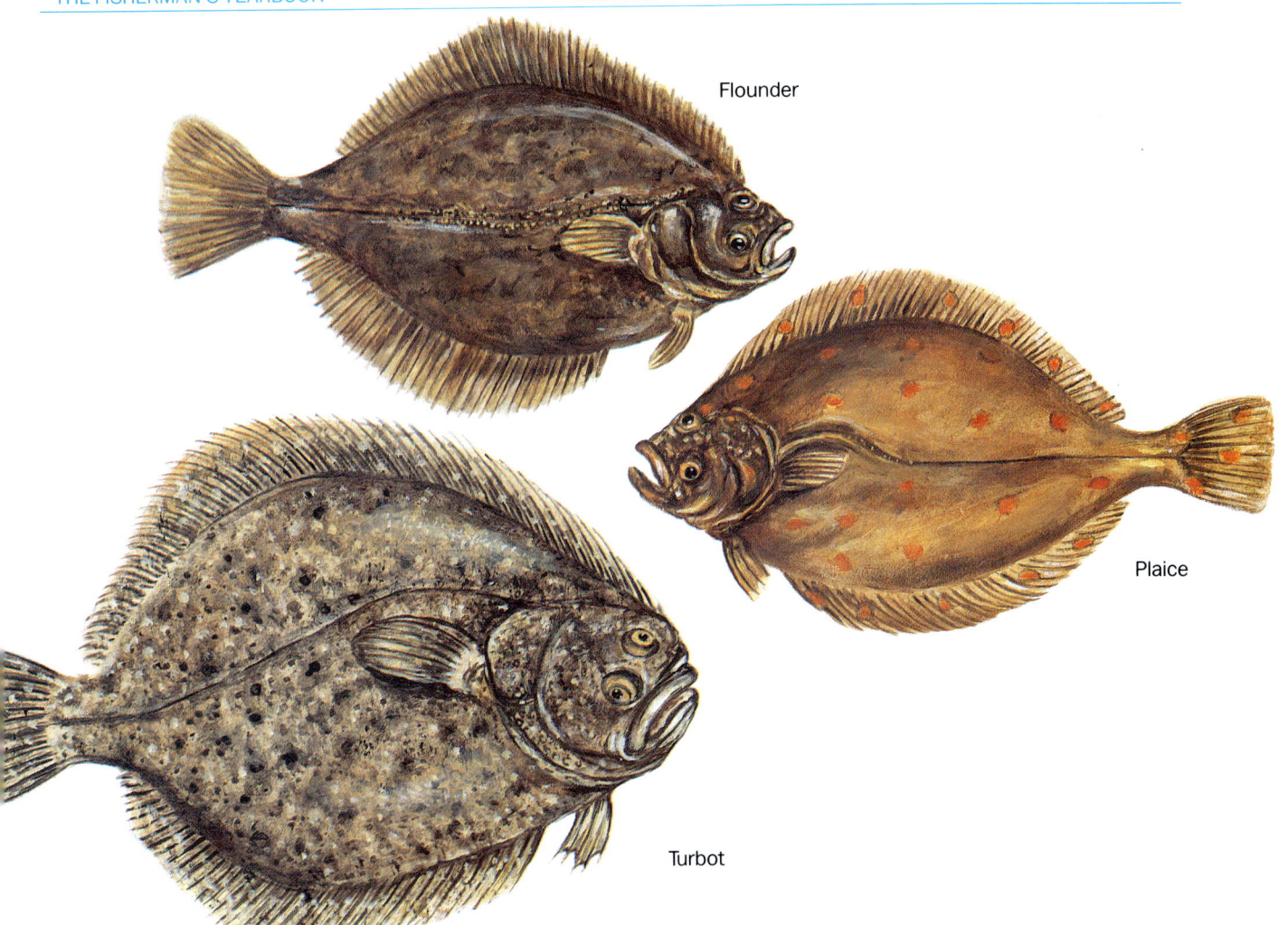

Flounder

Plaice

Turbot

SEA FISH

76

Bream, Black

Halibut

Sole

SEA FISH

Ling

Ballan wrasse

Garfish

SEA FISH

Monkfish

Common Skate

Thornback Ray

SEA FISH

Lesser-spotted Dogfish

Conger Eel

Tope

SEA FISH

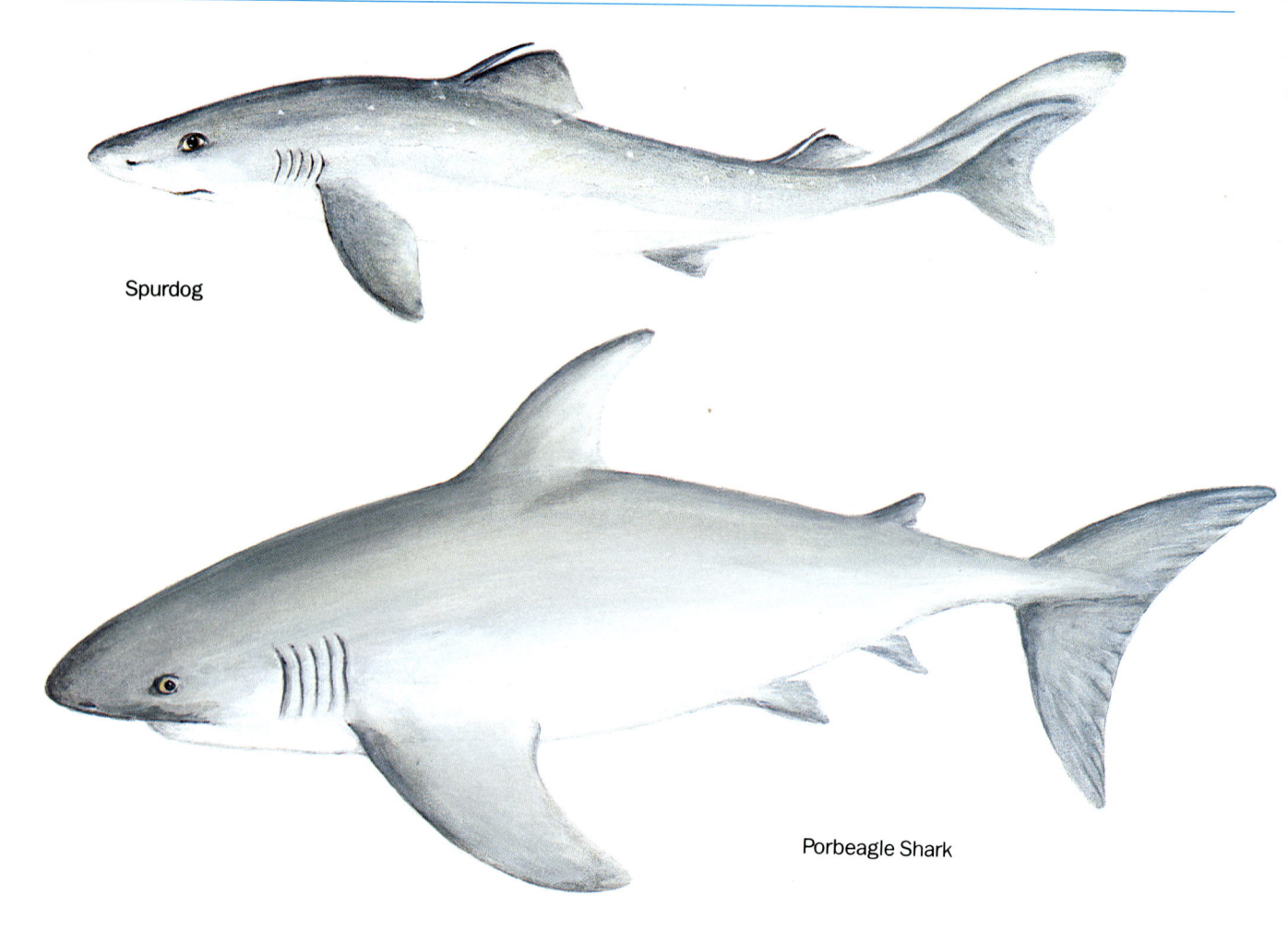

Spurdog

Porbeagle Shark

NEW TACKLE by JOHN WILSON

Every year countless new items of tackle appear on the British market together with many old ones, cosmetically upgraded. There is now such a glut of 'new' tackle available from carbon carp rods to lead-free shot, that the consumer is understandably bewildered. Choice, moreover, is made even more difficult by there being so many products which are more or less the same but marketed by different wholesalers under their own label.

Despite this, there are many original items of tackle of excellent design available this year. Space prohibits a full discussion of all these, and the following represents a review of but a small segment of the market. *(Note that prices, while accurate at the time of going to press, may increase without notice.)*

RODS

Freshwater Carbon/Match Rods

There has been little recent technical development in this category as carbon-fibre rods are now almost as thin and as light as they will ever be. Of numerous new models, the Sundridge Tackle 'Kevin Ashurst' Expert high modulous graphite match rod (retailing at £69.95), available in both 12 ft (3.6 m) and 13 ft (3.9 m), is particularly worth looking at. The distinctive maroon blank is nicely slim and has a superb snappy, yet forging action. It is whipped in red with Fuji match guides and has a half cork/half duplon, slim handle.

Coming down in price to the glass/carbon composite range, Shakespeare's 1843 Catcher Match Rods are excellent. The 12 ft (3.6 m) model — there are others in the range — retailing at £27.99, provides the beginner or youngster with a snappy-action float/match rod for use with light lines. The rod will also handle a 4 lb test line for tench and big bream.

Freshwater Specimen/Specialist Rods

There is probably now more choice in specimen-hunting rods — ranging from inexpensive glass/carbon composites to top quality carbon/kelvar specials — than in any other category.

At the lower end of the price scale, at £26.95, the new 1512 Series Carp Rod from Silstar offers exceptional value and proves that good-quality rods really are becoming cheaper. This composite eleven-footer (3.3 m) is suited to both carp and pike fishing with lines ranging from 7–11 lb test. Rings are ceramic-lined and the screw reel fitting is sandwiched between duplon grips.

In addition to their specialist range Ryobi Masterline have introduced the Super Specialist, a 12 ft (3.6 m) dark green carbon carp rod capable of handling lines in the 9–12 lb class, as the 2 lb curve suggests. Though powerful, it has a progressive action and a for giving tip for prising fish out of lily beds. Rings are ceramic-lined, and the matt black screw reel fitting has black duplon grips above and below. At £49.95 this versatile rod represents good value, as it can easily double as a pike rod. Casting range is 80 yards (73 m) with leads up to 2.25 oz (64 g).

From Sundridge there is no mistaking the distinctive emerald green, cross braid look of their new Expert Carp Rods. There are three rods in the range: two are 11 ft (3.3 m) with 1.75 lb and 2.25 lb test curves respectively, capable of handling most situations in distance fishing. The action is decidedly stiff, so these should suit 'long range' anglers. Both retail at £49.95 and come with ceramic-lined

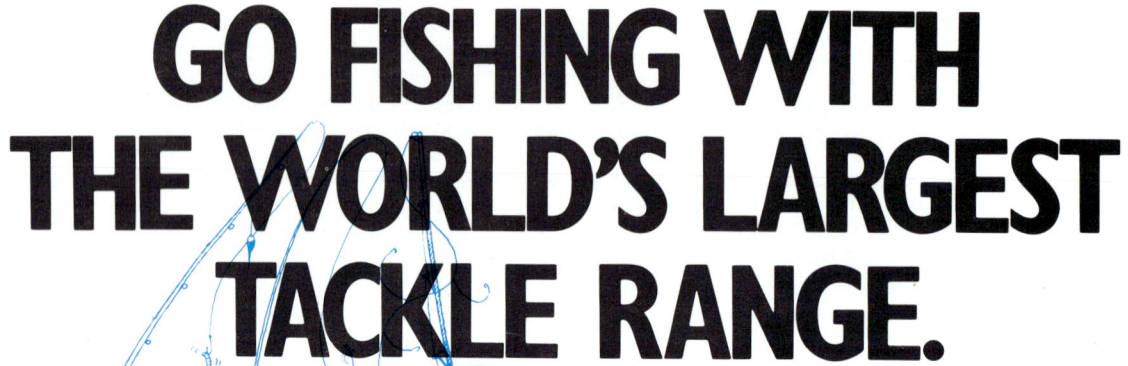

GO FISHING WITH THE WORLD'S LARGEST TACKLE RANGE.

Shakespeare®
SINCE 1897

Shakespeare Company, P.O. Box 1, Redditch, Worcs B98 8NQ.

rings and the usual Fuji/duplon handle arrangement.

The third model from Sundridge is a 12 ft (3.6 m) rod with a 2 lb test curve and an all-through action, ideal for close range work in snags. It retails at £59.95 and is identical to the others in the range.

From Ryobi Masterline comes a unique concept in lure fishing pike rods with the Barrie Rickards Master Pike 2. With this 9 ft (2.7 m) two-piece carbon beauty, you have the choice of either a handle suitable for using with fixed-spool reels or a cranked handle for multiplying reels. The cost is £35 for either style or, for an extra £14.99, you can have both. The tip section is considerably longer than the handle, ensuring that the spigot is low down the rod and allowing a full curve to develop for playing big fish. Recommended line strengths are from 8 – 12 lb test and any lure, from small spinners to large plugs, may be used. Rings are single leg ceramic-lined with black whippings tipped in red. The cranked handle version would suit a salmon-spinning enthusiast.

Daiwa's new range of eight VCC Specimen Rods (priced from £67.99 to £79.99) is sure to prove a winner. There is a choice of either 11 or 12 ft (3.3 or 3.6 m) models from 1.75 – 3 lb test curve. All models feature sixteen strand carbon braid, tube construction, and come fitted with speed-flow rings together with the usual Fuji reel fitting and small duplon collars. Rods in the middle to upper price range will meet every contingency in specimen hunting from zander to the biggest carp. All are two-piece, except the 12 ft (3.6 m) 2.5 lb test curve model which is three-piece.

Poles

Although carbon poles now corner the long rod market, there is still a demand for simple, inexpensive telescopic and take-apart glass-fibre poles. Youngsters especially cannot afford top prices and need something in the lower budget range to learn pole fishing.

An ideal beginner's pole is the Silstar 3000 Telescopic range. The 18 ft (6.3 m) length costs £15 and is ideal for general knockabout fishing. It will handle small fish on a light terminal rig and haul tench from lily beds.

Of the numerous lightweight carbon poles currently available, and there are hundreds, the new Majic S Range from D. A. M. Tackle offers particularly good value and is an ideal choice for beginner and ardent club angler alike. The 33 ft (10.8 m) version, retailing at £185 is rigid yet at 2.6 lb (1200 g) is very light. For an extra £14.95 there is an optional 1.4 m elasticated tip fitted with the new seymo rotating PTFE non-wearing tip, ready rigged with Milo elastic.

At the top of the price range, both Silstar and Shimano make unbelievably light, rigid poles. Pick of the vast Silstar range is the super-light 40 ft 10 in (12.5 m) 3095 Traverse X ten-section model made of radial graphite, weighing 2.6 lb (1220 g) and retailing at £595. More down to earth is the 36 ft 6 in (9.5m) version costing £399.

For the connoisseur Shimano have the ultimate pole design with their incredible TPCC-1400XX. A 45 ft 6 in (14 m) beauty, it weights just 2.3 lb (1070 g) and retails at a cool £2000.

Carbon Salmon Rods

Apart from poles, these are among the most expensive freshwater rods and with some makes you get little change from £200. Daiwa's new CF98 spigot ferruled salmon fly rod range, however, is very competitively priced. The '98' refers to a 98 per cent carbon content so you know the blank is sound. Prices vary from £69.99 for a three-piece 12 ft (3.6 m) rod which takes lines in the 8 – 9 lb range, to £115 for the four-piece 18 ft (5.4 m) rod which takes 10 – 12 lb lines. Dynaflo rings are used throughout and the finish is typical Daiwa quality.

Beachcasting Rods

If you are looking for a real budget-priced carbon phenolic (carbon/glass composite) beachcaster, then the Sundridge 12 ft (3.6 m) Technik which cast 5 leads in the 4 – 8 oz range is just the thing. It has ceramic-lined rings throughout on a rapid taper blank and retails at £32.95.

Freshwater Reels

New from the reliable and famous Mitchell range comes a fine pair of freshwater reels, the 2140 RD and the 2165 RD. Not as gimmicky as reels from the Far East with ball races, bronze pinions and a stainless bale arm, these Mitchells are made to last. They feature sterndrags, skirted spools and the famous Mitchell guarantee for life. The 2140 RD holds 200 yards (180 m) of 8 lb test and costs £22.95. The 2165 RD holds 240 yards (216 m) of 12 lb test and costs £25.95.

The most noticeable feature of Shimano's new Biomaster reels, and there are six models in the range, is the long tapered, graphite spool and compact body. Ideal for the long-range carp fishing fraternity, these new reels have two-speed oscillation across the spool giving perfect cross-wind line lay, hence long casting. But they are not cheap. The 3500 carp-sized model costs £66.90 and the 4500, an excellent beachcasting reel, costs £74.90.

Long awaited by match fishermen, the new Abu Garcia 1044 Syncromatch closed-faced reel is already winning admirers. It has all the quality of past Abu favourites with a distinctly modern styling. The drag system is silky smooth with the drag knob on the handle and there is an optional anti-reverse. The 1044 retails at £49.99 and comes with two spools.

Retailing at £29.99, Daiwa's new Harrier 123M is the cheapest ambidexterous closed-face reel around. It has no drag system so will suit those who like to play fish by back winding. The gear ratio is 4:1 and the body is of graphite construction. The spool is interchangeable with the 120M reel.

For all pike and salmon artificial lure enthusiasts who would like a left-hand wind multiplier, Abu have finally obliged with their new 6001C (LH). This lovely little reel casts like a dream with lines in the 9–10 lb test range and, like all Abu multipliers, has a very smooth clutch. At £79.99 it is not cheap, but then real quality seldom is.

Completely new in design from Leeda Tackle is a family of handsome fly reels, the LC Reels. There are three models. The lightweight 60 retails at £19.50; the regular 80 at £19.95 and the kingsize 100 at £20.50. All prices include a spare spool which simply moves on and off a sprocket by means of a push button. There is also an adjustable check with quick scale read.

Sea Reels

One of the drawbacks with high gear fixed-spool sea reels is that whilst reeling in empty line is a pleasure, playing a biggish fish, or trying to wind in a clump of weed, certainly is not. What is needed is a reel that will enable you to quickly retrieve one moment and switch to a low gear the next. The new Ryobi T/S5 does just that. Simply by flicking the power shift lever, situated at the rear, gear ratio

ONLY ONE FLY LINE IS GUARANTEED NOT TO CRACK

Buy one, and say goodbye to cracked lines. **RRP £26.90**
SEND NOW FOR FULL DETAILS ON ALL AIRFLO LINES – FLY FISHING TECHNOLOGY LTD., UNITS 3 & 4, INDUSTRIAL ESTATE, BRECON, POWYS, WALES. TELEPHONE: 0874 4448.

'KINGFISHER'

Import – Export – Manufacturer of Specialist Fishing Equipment

Before   **After**   Can also be used on full brolly camps

BROLLY POLE CONVERSIONS

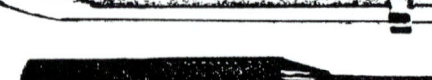

BOILIE NEEDLE WITH UNIQUE 'HAIR SAFE'

36 LOMBARD STREET, HORTON KIRBY, KENT DA4 9DF

* OBTAINABLE FROM YOUR LOCAL TACKLE SHOP *

is immediately changed from a rapid 5-2:1 to 3-0:1. The TS also has a silent anti-reverse gear. It is ambidexterous and the spool holds 280 yards (252 m) of 20 lb test. The reel will handle anything from dabs to conger and costs £69.95.

Best of the modern multipliers is the new Triton Speedmaster from Shimano, a super high-speed beachcasting reel with an all-graphite corrosion-free body. It features two ball-bearing races, a ball-bearing titanium drag system and a light-weight alloy spool. There are two different sized models: the TSM2 FSC holds 330 yards (297 m) of 14 lb line and retails at £99.99, while the big LD50H takes 380 yards (342 m) of 25 lb test and costs £104.99. With either of these two reels you could handle anything swimming offshore in British and most foreign waters.

LINES

Nothing oustandingly new in lines to report, except that Maxima line is now available in green, in addition to the existing slate grey. It is available from 2 lb test, and 100 yards (90 m) of 6 lb test, for example, retails at £2.95.

LANDING NETS

The new Apex range of triangular nets from Efgeeco is a vast improvement on the now outdated alloy arm type. The Apex has arms of carbon phenolic held apart by a strong spreader block with standard thread. The net is good quality nylon, knotless minnow mesh and, like the frame, black. There are five models to choose from ranging from 24 in (60 cm) and retailing at £13.95 to the giant 42 in (105 cm) specimen net at £24.95, capable of engulfing anything swimming in British freshwater.

SCALES

Bigger and bigger carp are being caught these days. This is presumably one of the reasons why the Avon Scale Company have added a new model to their famous clock dial range. It measures up to 40 lb (18 kg) with 1 oz (28 g) divisions and retails at £29.95. The new Mark 7 model has four revolutions of the dial, each indicated by a colour coded band to avoid any mistake being made.

Also new is a large clock scale from Reuben Heaton, suitable for both sea and freshwater specimen fish as it registers up to 60 lb (27 kg) with 1 oz (28g) divisions and it indicates the weight in metric as well as imperial units. This strongly-built, easy-to-read scale retails at £59.95

MULTI DROPPERED LEADER

Attention all fly fishermen who hate tying their own droppered leaders! Your prayers have been answered by Masterline's new Multi-Droppered Leader Dispenser. A spool containing 75 yards (67.5 m) of either 3 lb or 6 lb line has 4 in (10 cm) droppers tied every 3 ft 3 in (1 m), providing twenty two-droppered leaders to fish three flies on each cast. The 'Monosafe' dispenser incorporates a cutter which both cuts the line and holds it securely until the next leader is required. A real breakthrough to the game angler, each dispenser costs £5.75

PREMADE BAITS

The sale of ready-made carp baits is big business and the number of products available is expanding each year. New in presentation this year the Catchum Pro-mix Boilies, available in handy snap-lid tubs with a choice of mouth-watering (for the carp) flavours. Each tub has a colour-coded lid and contains around 300 baits for £3.70.

BAIT PUMP

Looking very much like a stirrup pump and better known in Australia as a 'Yabbie Pump', the Alvey Super Suction Bait Pump has been on sale down under for many years. It will be interesting to see, therefore, whether its magic of persuading lugworms and ragworms to be sucked out of their burrows will work as effectively in this country. It is not, however, cheap, retailing at £31.95, but then neither are lugworms per 100.

SPECIMEN-HUNTING LUGGAGE

Large ruck-type bags are now very much in vogue with big fish anglers, so the new Bob Church Giant Specimen Hunter's Ruck Bag is bound to be a success. Retailing at £42.25 it is capable of holding virtually anything you may need. There are numerous pockets, including a padded camera pocket, and it sensibly includes a shoulder harness.

The Wanderer waistcoat.

RECLINING BEDCHAIRS

All ardent night-fishers like to while away the hours of darkness in comfort, so two new products from Fox International are bound to be popular. Retailing at £49.90, the new non-adjustable bedchair is made of non-reflecting green aero grade tubular aluminium and weighs 8 lb (3.6 kg). Opened, it measures 75 in (1.8 m) in length by 22.5 in (55 cm) wide.

For the man who does not mind what he spends, the Super Deluxe Adjusta Level Bedchair at £139.90 seems to have everything. Finished in dark green sixteen-gauge aero aluminium, it has adjustable legs front and back and a fully adjustable canvas cover incorporating a 1.5 in (3.75 cm) thick foam core. Opened it measures 76½ in (1.9 m) by 26 in (65 cm).

CLOTHING

The Wanderer Waistcoat from Ryobi Masterline has enough pockets to suit the game and coarse fisherman alike — a dual purpose for which it was specifically designed. Tailored from hardwearing olive corduroy and incorporating a thermal lining for all-year-round use, this longer-than-normal waistcoat is stylishly cut and has shoulder epaulettes. The large double-zipped pocket in the lower back will hold two two-pint (1 l) bait-boxes, a loaf of bread, a bag of boilies or a box of flies, spinners or plugs. There are special tabs for forceps, a scissor pocket and two D-rings. At £39.50 it is bound to be a hit with anglers who prefer the wandering approach.

For the angler who goes afloat regularly, how about a waistcoat with built-in buoyancy? Crewsavers have produced such a garment in olive green and retailing at £47.50. It complies fully with British Standard 3595 and, with so many pockets, it is also well-suited to the needs of game fishermen.

POLARISED SUNGLASSES

While many companies selling Polaroids have gone distinctly upmarket with price increases, it's nice to see that Shakespeare have done the opposite. Their new Opti Shield Glasses, available in matt black or brown frames and either amber or smoke lenses, offer unbelievable value at £5.99.

BOARD GAME

'Get Hooked' by Kingfisher Games Ltd. is the first sensible and authentic fishing board game to be produced. This lively dice game can be played by two to four participants and the instructions on many of the playing cards offer sensible fishing advice. So, not only is the game fun to play, it is also instructive. The retail price is £19.99.

THE FISHERMAN'S YEARBOOK — NEW TACKLE — 89

SHIMANO

Quality isn't expensive.

The same precision, technology and commitment that go into our world-famous Baitrunners are standard in all Shimano reels. The secret is our super ball bearing races and precision-cut gearing which will give years of faithful service. You may pay a little more for Shimano but in the long run the extra service will repay itself time and time again. Call into your authorised dealer and see the complete range for yourself.

CARBOMATIC

Titanium/Graphite Body · 3 Ball Bearing Races · 2 Extra Spare Spools on Sizes 1000/2000/3000 · Rear Dual Drag System · S.I.C. Ceramic Line Roller · Bio Grip Stem · Silent Anti Reverse · Push Button Graphite Spools

PRICES FROM £39.90

CUSTOM GT

No Fail Bail · Pre-set Clutch System · Graphite/Titanium Body · Push Button Graphite Spools · Bio Grip Stem · Silent Anti Reverse · 3 Ball Bearing Races · S.I.C. Ceramic Roller Guide · Ball Arm Springs · Guaranteed Never to Fail · Left or Right Hand Wind

PRICES FROM £32.90

SGT MASTER DRAG

Titanium/Graphite Body · S.I.C. Ceramic Line Roller · Ball Bearing · Sensitive Rear Fighting Drag · Left or Right Hand Wind · Bio Grip Stem · Spare Spools · Silent Anti Reverse

PRICES FROM £27.90

To see the precision, technology and commitment, call in at your authorised dealer or send £1 cheque/PO for coat patch and colour catalogue.

SHIMANO (Europe) GmbH, Unit B2 Lakeside Technology Park, Phoenix Way, Swansea Enterprise Park, Llansamlet, Swansea SA7 9EH.

John Wilson's Guide to UK Tackle Dealers

England

AVON

Veals of Bristol,
61 Old Market Street,
Bristol.
Tel: 0272 20790.

Weston Angling Centre,
25 Locking Road,
Weston-Super-Mare
Tel: 0934 31140

BEDFORDSHIRE

Dixons,
95 Tavistock Street,
Bedford.
Te: 0234 67145.

Leslie's,
74 Park Street,
Luton.
Tel: 0582 35740.

BERKSHIRE

Thomas Turner's,
Whitley Street,
Reading.
Tel: 0734 874367.

Reading Angling Centre,
69 Northumberland Avenue,
Reading.
Tel: 0734 872219.

BUCKINGHAMSHIRE

Cox the Saddler Ltd.,
23 High Street,
Chesham.
Tel: 0494 771340.

Lakes,
26 Church Street,
and
28 Stratford Road,
Milton Keynes.
Tel: 0908 312553/313142.

CAMBRIDGESHIRE

Beecrofts,
207 Cherry Hinton Road,
Cambridge.
Tel: 0223 49010.

St Ives Angling Centre,
5 Crown Street,
St Ives.
Tel: 0480 301903

CHANNEL ISLANDS

P. & J. Tackle,
7 Beresford Market,
St Helier,
Jersey.

Tackle & Accessories,
32 The Market,
St Peter Port,
Guernsey.

CHESHIRE

Edgeley Sports & Fishing Depot,
145/147 Castle Street,
Stockport.
Tel: 061 480 2511.

Barlow of Bond Street,
47 Bond Street,
Macclesfield.
Tel: 0625 619935.

CLEVELAND

Angler's Corner,
121/123 Abingdon Road,
Middlesborough.
Tel: 0642 313103.

Cleveland Angling Centre,
22 Westbury Street,
Thornaby.
Tel: 0642 67700

CORNWALL

J. Bray & Sons,
The Quay,
Looe.
Tel: 050 36 2504

Ken's Tackle
9 Beachfield Court,
The Promenade,
Penzance.
Tel: 0736 61969.

CUMBRIA

The Complete Angler,
4 King Street,
Whitehaven.
Tel: 0946 5322.

Carlisle Angling Centre,
105 Lowther Street,
Carlisle.
Tel: 0228 24035.

DERBYSHIRE

Artisan Angling,
141 London Road,
Derby.
Tel: 0332 40981

Fosters of Ashbourne,
32 St John's Street,
Ashbourne.
Tel: 0335 43155.

DEVON

Exeter Angling Centre,
Smythen Street,
Off Market Street,
Exeter.
Tel: 0392 36404.

Ted Tuckerman's Angling Centre,
141 St Mary's Church Road,
Torquay.
Tel: 0803 36216.

DORSET

Davis Tackle,
75 Bargates,
Christchurch.
Tel: 0202 485169.

Poole Angling Centre,
19 High Street,
Poole.
Tel: 0202 674409.

DURHAM

W. P. Adams,
42 Dore Street,
Darlington.
Tel: 0325 468069

Anglers' Services,
45 Claypath,
Durham.
Tel: 0385 47584.

ESSEX

Jetty Anglers,
47 Eastern Esplanade,
Southend-on-Sea.
Tel: 0702 611826.

Romford Angling Centre,
209–211 North Street,
Romford.
Tel: 0708 763370.

GLOUCESTERSHIRE

D & J Sports,
71 Crickdale Street,
Cirencester.
Tel: 0285 2229

The Tackle Shop,
56 Church Street,
Tewkesbury.
Tel: 0684 293234.

HAMPSHIRE

John Conning Sports & Tackle,
8 Portsmouth Road,
Woolston,
Southampton.

Two Guys Ltd.,
27 Burnaby Close,
Basingstoke.
Tel: 0256 64981.

HEREFORD & WORCESTER

Mal Storey,
129 Sutton Road,
Kidderminster.
Tel: 0562 745221.

Powell's,
28 Mount Pleasant,
Redditch.
Tel: 0527 62669.

HERTFORDSHIRE

Alan Brown,
118 Nightingale Road,
Hitchin.
Tel: 0462 59918.

Simpsons of Turnford,
Turnford,
Cheshunt.
Tel: 0992 468799.

HUMBERSIDE

Barry's of Goole Ltd.,
316/318 Beverley Road,
Hull.
Tel: 0482 448846.

Mallard Angling Supplies,
5 Harbour Road,
Bridlington.
Tel: 0262 73103.

ISLE OF WIGHT

Scotts,
11 Lugely Street,
Newport.
Tel: 0983 522115

KENT

Ron Edwards,
50 High Street,
Herne Bay.
Tel: 02273 72517.

Kent Angling,
86 King Street,
Ramsgate.
Tel: 0843 592924.

LANCASHIRE

Carters,
Church Street,
Preston.
Tel: 0772 53476.

Gerry's of Morecambe,
156 Heysham Road,
Morecambe.
Tel: 0524 422146.

LEICESTERSHIRE

Bennets,
Market Place,
Mount Sorrel,
Loughborough.
Tel: 0533 302818.

TACKLE DEALERS

Marks & Marlow,
39 Tudor Street,
Leicester.
Tel: 0533 537714.

LINCOLNSHIRE

The Newport Tackle Shop,
85 Newport,
Lincoln.
Tel: 0522 25861.

J. Morley Sports Ltd.,
5 Wide Bargate,
Boston.
Tel: 0205 62544

LONDON AREA

Acton Angling Centre,
187 Old Park Road,
East Acton.
Tel: 01-743 3381.

Croydon Angling Centre,
65 London Road,
Croydon.
Tel: 01-688 7564.

Don's of Edmonton,
239 Fore Street,
Edmonton.
Tel: 01-807 5396.

Gerry's of Wimbledon,
170 The Broadway,
Wimbledon SW19
Tel: 01-542 7792.

John's Tackle Box,
244 Woodhouse Road,
Friern Barnet.
Tel: 01-368 8799.

Frames Fishing Tackle,
202 The Broadway,
Hendon.
Tel: 01-202 0264.

MERSEYSIDE

Johnson's Angling Centre,
469 Rice Lane,
Liverpool.
Tel: 051-525 5574

Virgo Marine Angling Centre,
114 Seaview Road,
Wallasey.
Tel: 051 6304543.

NORFOLK

John's Tackle Den,
16 Bridewell Alley,
Norwich.
Tel: 0603 614114.

Lathams,
Potter Heigham.
Tel: (0692) 670388.

NORTHAMPTONSHIRE

Russ's,
St Leonard's Road,
Northampton.
Tel: 0604 764847.

Gilders,
The Old Bakehouse,
Ketteringham.
Tel: 0536 514509.

NOTTINGHAMSHIRE

Gerry's of Nottingham,
276 Denham Road,
Radford,
Nottingham.
Tel: 0602 781695.

Walkers of Trowell,
9–15 Nottingham Road,
Trowell.
Tel: 0602 301816.

OXFORDSHIRE

Dell's Tackle,
Cowley Road,
Oxford.
Tel: 0865 711410.

Ian Heyden,
2 East St Helen Street,
Abingdon.
Tel: 0235 26579.

SALOP

G. Forrest,
2 Wyle Cop,
Shrewsbury.
Tel: 0743 56778.

Stuart Williams,
5 Underhill Street,
Bridgnorth.
Tel. 074 62 2832.

SOMERSET

A. B. Pearce,
Street Angling Centre,
Street.
Tel. 0458 47830.

Peter Thyer,
3 Church Street,
Highbridge.
Tel: 0278 786934.

STAFFORDSHIRE

Pickering's of Burslem,
4 William Clowes Street,
Stoke-on-Trent.
Tel: 0782 814941

Tony Scott,
30 Borough Road,
Burton-on-Trent.
Tel: 0283 48540.

SUFFOLK

The Tackle Box,
Acton Square,
Sudbury.
Tel: 0787 312118.

Ipswich Angling Centre,
199 Felixstowe Road,
Ipswich.
Tel: 0473 78004.

SURREY

Guildford Angling Centre,
93/94 Haydon Place,
Guildford.
Tel: 0483 506333.

Molesey Angling,
4 Hampton Court Parade,
East Molesey.
Tel. 01-941 6633.

SUSSEX

Ken Dunman Ltd.,
2 Marine Place,
Worthing.
Tel: 0903 39802

Hastings Angling Centre,
33–35 The Bourne,
Hastings.
Tel: 0424 432148.

TYNE AND WEAR

Bagnall & Kirkwood Ltd.,
52 Grey Street,
Newcastle.
Tel: 091 2325873.

Coast & Country Sports,
3 Derwent Street,
Sunderland.
Tel: 0783 659666.

WARWICKSHIRE

Bailey's Fishing Tackle,
30 Emscote Road,
Warwick.
Tel: 0926 491984.

Ashbys,
182 Lythalls Lane,
Coventry.
Tel: 0203 687900.

WEST MIDLANDS

Harold Greenway & Sons,
1010 Chester Road,
Pype Hayes,
Birmingham.
Tel: 021-747 6838.

Ken Austen & Son Ltd.,
2 Alfred Street,
West Bromwich.
Tel: 021-553 0392.

WILTSHIRE

Swindon Angling Centre,
5 Sheppard Street,
Swindon.
Tel: 0793 619909

Wests,
32 Roundstone Street,
Trowbridge.
Tel: 02214 5472.

YORKSHIRE

Bennets of Sheffield,
1–5 Stanley Street,
Sheffield.
Tel: 0742 756756.

Kirkgate Anglers,
95 Kirkgate,
Leeds.
Tel: 0532 4344880.

WALES

CLWYD

Angler's Den,
29 Queen Street,
Rhyl.
Tel: 0745 54765.

Caldwells,
19 Henblas Street,
Wrexham.
Tel: 0978 265179

DYFED

Angler's Corner,
80 Station Road,
Llanelli.
Tel: 0554 773981

B. Jones
3 Queen Street,
Aberystwyth.
Tel: 0970 7451.

GWENT

Fussel's Sports,
53 Cross Street,
Abergavenny.
Tel: 0873 3333.

Pill Angling Services,
160 Commercial Road,
Newport.
Tel: 0633 211710

GWYNEDD

Ron Edwards,
6 Dean Street,
Bangor.
Tel: 0248 2811.

MID-GLAMORGAN

Tony's Tackle,
18 Castle Street,
Caerphilly.
Tel: 0222 885409.

POWYS

Sue Burgess Ltd.,
The Industrial Estate,
Brecon.
Tel: 0874 4448.

WEST GLAMORGAN

Capston House,
Beach Street,
Swansea.
Tel: 0792 54756.

Tackle & Bait,
149 Windsor Street,
Neath.
Tel: 0639 54148.

SOUTH GLAMORGAN

A. Bale & Son Ltd.,
3 Frederick Street,
Cardiff.
Tel: 0222 29929.

Scotland

BORDERS

Stothart's Tackle Shop,
6 High Street,
Hawick
Tel: 0450 72234

CENTRAL

D. Crockart & Son,
47 King Street,
Stirling.
Tel: 0786 73443.

DUMFRIES AND GALLOWAY

M. Pattie,
103 Queensbury Street,
Dumfries.
Tel: 0387 52891.

FIFE

J. Wilson & Sons,
169 South Street,
St Andrews.

GRAMPIAN

David's,
Market Square,
Stonehaven

HIGHLAND REGION

R. Ross,
Main Street,
Lairg.
Tel: 0549 2239.

LOTHIAN

John Dickson & Son,
21 Frederick Street,
Edinburgh
Tel: 031 225 4218.

SHETLAND

Stove & Smith,
97 Commercial Street,
Lerwick.

TAYSIDE

Shotcast Ltd.,
8 Whitehall Crescent,
Dundee.
Tel: 0382 25621.

WESTERN ISLES

The Sports Shop,
6 North Beach Street,
Stornaway,
Isle of Lewis.
Tel: 0851 5464.

J. S. Morrison,
Tarbet,
Isle of Harris.

NORTHERN IRELAND

ANTRIM

D. McKeown,
155 Moira Road,
Lisburn.
Tel: 084-62 81275/81403.

ARMAGH

Sidney Beckett,
The Sports Shop,
High Street,
Lurgan.
Tel: 076-22 23352.

BELFAST

Kenneth Rankin Ltd.,
131 Royal Avenue,
Belfast.
Tel: 0232 222657.

DOWN

Comber Sports Centre Ltd.,
18 Castle Street,
Comber.
Tel: 0247 872846.

FERMANAGH

Lakeland Tackle,
Sligo Road,
Enniskillen.
Tel: 0365 23774.

TYRONE

Tyrone Tackle,
Market Place,
Omagh.
Tel: 0662 44827.

THE SEA ANGLING YEAR
by MIKE MILLMAN

'The saltwater anglers' year', writes Mike Millman, 'follows a predictable pattern and has undergone very little change beyond a widening of opportunity since fishing with rod and line began in earnest over a century ago.'

Shore Fishing

Cod, whiting, dabs and flounder are the dominant species in January, February and early March. The dedicated shore man longs for cold clear nights when beach shingle glistens with frost and crackles underfoot. In these conditions, the above species are well within casting range and eager to feed on a variety of baits. Lugworm can be found in sand and mud in many places around the coast and lugworm probably accounts for seventy per cent of all fish taken from the shore during winter. In south and south-west England king ragworm and frozen peeler and soft-back crab also play starring roles. Squid strip is also used extensively, both on its own or as an ingredient in a cocktail-bait.

The distribution of cod has increased dramatically during the past ten years and is no longer the prerogative of anglers working the beaches of the east coast, the northern flanks of England

Last light on a tidal river for flounder or bass fishing.

The British Record flounder, (shore 5 lb. 3 oz.) River Teign, Devon.

and Scottish waters. Today, fine sport is available as far west as Dorset, Devon and Cornwall and many fish of specimen size come from a variety of marks in these areas.

Whiting is very prolific inshore during winter and fine catches are made from beaches and rock stations. Dorset's Chesil Beach has the distinction of the British Shore Record for a fish of 4 lb (1.8 kg), hooked at Abbotsbury.

Winter is also the time for plump dabs and flounder, with voracious bull huss always on the look-out for a meal. The tidal rivers of south-west England offer the biggest winter flounder and are pursued with vigour by thousands of 'flattie' enthusiasts.

Each year Devon's River Teign produces flounder of record breaking class – fish in excess of 5 lb (2 kg). In addition, many thousands half that size, but still big compared with the average weights in other parts of the country, are also recorded each season.

By the end of March, flounder have deserted the beaches and tidal rivers and plaice now begin to feature in catches. The fish is widely distributed, but marks off Scotland and south-west England have the edge for prize-winning specimens. With the spring come mackerel, first making their appearance at marks washed by the slightly warmer waters of the western English Channel. Float fishing with ragworm is very

Specimen cod taken off the Cornish coast.

SEA ANGLING

popular, particularly with young anglers enjoying the Easter break from school.

With the arrival of warmer days, grey mullet, the aptly-named ghosts of English waters, haunt estuaries and harbours and extend far into tidal river systems. This most infuriating but fascinating of species stays within range until mid-October, providing the patient and dedicated angler with the greatest challenge. Ground-baiting for an hour or more before a light float rig is cast into the water is essential and, even then, there is no guarantee that the crafty fish will strike at a tiny hook of however cunningly concealed. So close is its behaviour to that of many equally difficult-to-catch freshwater species that it is a great favourite with holidaying coarse fishermen.

From late spring through to early winter the bass, perhaps the most challenging and exciting quarry of all, arrives on the open beaches and in the maze of deep gullies which make up much of the coastline of southern and south-west England. Bass are most active at night and lines of pressure lamps, creating dots of light in the blackness of lonely beaches, testify to its popularity.

The British Record shore-caught mackerel of 5 lb. 11 oz. Berry Head Quarry, Devon (left). (Right) A mullet caught at dawn near Hannaford Point.

Bass is the most ferocious fighter of all, testing man and tackle to the limit. It is often said that a bass weighing double figures is a fish of a lifetime and there are few who would disagree. Bass hit hard and will continue fighting until a wide-mouthed net settles the encounter – although a high percentage will break tackle and live to battle again. Squid, mackerel, marine worms, sand eel and crab are the top baits.

The most predictable species of all in summer and autumn is the ballan wrasse. A dweller of deep rock gullies where a jungle of kelp weed sways endlessly with the movement of the sea, the wrasse is tough, uncompromising and a great sporting fish. Give it quarter and the game is finished before it is begun, but the memory of the snatch transmitted to the rod tip as the bait is engulfed, lingers for some time.

Equipped with leathery jaws and teeth, the wrasse's mouth is designed to crush crustaceans and limpets. Anglers with an enthusiasm for the species ledger hard-back, peeler and soft-back crab.

Wrasse are widely distributed and found where there is rock and weed, but the best specimen hunting is on the Welsh, Irish, south-west England and Channel Islands' coasts. The biggest fish are usually taken in areas not fished extensively. A prime example is the

An 11.5lb bass from Eddystone Reef.

A 5 lb. ballan wrasse (left), and (right), a good Thornback ray from the River Tamar.

coastline of Alderney in the Channel Islands which offers enormous potential. It is likely that before long a British Record could be established here.

From May to October thornback and small-eyed ray are popular quarries along the south coast of England and at marks on the coast of west Wales. Blonde and cuckoo varieties of ray provide steady sport mostly after dark on the Channel Islands' coastline, and Northern Ireland also offers considerable potential.

Summer is a good time to fish for pollack on rough ground. Cornwall's soaring headlands, swept by deep Atlantic water, fish well and pollack are also common in Irish waters.

Throughout the year conger eel features in shore catches, although the best period is from June to November. Very large fish are taken after dark (when you might also encounter the bull huss, a species of dogfish which grows large and has an appetite to match) at rock marks, notable among them being several places on Portland Bill in Dorset. Here fifty-pounders (23 kg) have come writhing out of the depths to provide even further excitement for those trying to retrieve 6 ft (1.8 m) of muscle on to dry land.

Conger are one of the most accessible of species, taking up residence far from the sea in tidal rivers. They are also commonly found in harbours.

With the arrival of October, flounder begin to reappear on the beaches and enter tidal rivers, their numbers building steadily to provide fine fishing throughout the winter.

Conger and ling.

Bass and turbot from the Skerries Banks.

Boat Fishing

Pollack, coalfish and ling fill the thoughts of boat anglers during the first months of the year. Wrecks lying in deep water, many miles from land, are a specimen hunter's dream and yield hundreds of huge fish. The principal port for long-range charter operations during the winter are Plymouth, Salcombe, Dartmouth and Brixham in Devon, and Whitby on the North Yorkshire coast where Weighmasters are constantly called on to check record-breaking contenders.

Although the heyday of wreck fishing is now past due to intense commercial netting of wrecks and the removal of tonnes of fish, it is still possible for a ten-man team of experienced anglers to return from a twelve-hour trip with 1000lb (454 kg) of fish. This hectic and demanding sport lasts until mid-March when the roe-swollen females spawn. Within a matter of days the great shoals of pollack and coalfish break up and the survivors return to the depths of the Atlantic.

As the wreck predators leave, plaice begin to arrive in the coastal waters and nowhere is rod and line fishing better than on the tide-swept Skerries Banks lying off the south Devon coast. The first fish appear in the middle of February and, by the end of March, the charter fleet working out of the historic port of Dartmouth is returning with an average of fifty fish a day.

Although there is not a 'run' as such, the much-prized turbot is available from April on the Skerries and the shingle banks of Lannacombe Bay, a few miles to the west. Big-flattie enthusiasts have set national records in these areas. Excellent fishing for a variety of flatfish species is also enjoyed on the Shambles Banks, a few miles off Dorset and the Varne, at the eastern end of the Channel.

In spring, bass start to come within range. Principal areas include the Eddystone and Manacles Reefs in Cornish waters, the Needles area of the Solent, and Pan Sands off the Kent coast where the British Record was set in 1987. The Race of Alderney, separating the island from the coast of France, also offers the finest of bass fishing. This great predator remains in coastal waters throughout the summer and early winter before disappearing to warmer waters.

The tope makes its presence felt in mid-April, particularly in the waters of the Solent and off the coasts of Essex and west Wales. Tope fishing usually hits a peak at the end of May and throughout June. This is the time when pollack hunt over rough ground where there is a good depth of water. Cornish reefs, between 6–10 miles (10–16 km) offshore and those in Channel Island and Irish waters offer the very best of sport.

In summer, reefs and wrecks can be fished for conger with considerable success. Offshore wrecks are the prime targets for devoted conger hunters intent on smashing the current British Record of 109 lb 6 oz (49.609 kg). Where there is deep, dark water, the nocturnal eel feeds quite well, even when the surface of the sea is glittering with sunlight. After-dark fishing is best in the shallows. The conger holes-up in harbours and tidal rivers and its distribution is very

A giant conger taken from an offshore wreck.

wide, with most of the really large specimens coming from English Channel marks.

At the other end of the size scale is the whiting, a very prolific species available through much of the year but with catches peaking during the colder months. Its near relative, the cod, is widespread during winter and excellent fishing is enjoyed by anglers working from ports in Scotland, Northern Ireland and the north-east and east coasts of England. Big catches are made at wrecks in the deeps of the English Channel during the summer, but the heavy-weights appear later in the year.

Haddock fishing is best around the Isle of Man and northern flanks of England.

A relatively recent development in boat fishing is the long-range extended charter between one of several south-west ports and Guernsey's St Peter Port. Sailing from the Devon coast in the early morning, the boat passes the separation zone of the Channel after a four-hour trip. Here the party of anglers, which may number up to ten, settle down for a session over one of the many wrecks – victims of two World Wars and the elements – which litter this part of the Channel. The middle zones of the English Channel hold more than 400 wrecks and have become huge holding areas.

After an intense period of fishing with many species of predator taking baits,

Charter boats for anglers at Plymouth.

SEA ANGLING

Mike Millman with a fine 252 lb Porbeagle

the boat heads for St Peter Port. Here the group usually stays for a couple of days before returning to Devon. On the journey home another mid-zone wreck is fished.

Charters of this type are rapidly gaining popularity and top skippers who specialise in this type of charter have opened up a new and rewarding dimension to sea fishing. In the not-too-distant future large craft with on-board sleeping accommodation and full cooking facilities will appear on the British angling scene, increasing the range of operations even further.

The boat anglers' year would not be complete without reference to sharks. In April porbeagle, a close relative of the great white shark of *Jaws* fame, begins to hunt over the reefs within a mile of the north Cornwall and Devon coasts. Crackington Haven and Hartland Point have superb shark fishing which lasts throughout the summer and well into the autumn. Porbeagle can also be found, together with the spectacular thresher, in the waters surrounding the Isle of Wight and the Channel Islands. The world record for porbeagle and most of the IGFA World Line Class Records have been set by British anglers fishing home waters.

With the onset of summer, blue shark migrate with the warm Gulf Stream into British waters and provide steady sport until the first weeks of October. Most blues average 45lb (20kg), but one in thirty will be double that weight and the number of 100kg (45kg) plus specimens reported has shown a healthy increase in recent years. This is largely due to the convservation programme of 'put them back alive' promoted by the Shark Angling Club of Great Britain, which has its headquarters at the Cornish port of Looe.

Warm, settled weather usually provides the best shark fishing and the best marks are off Wales, Northern Ireland and throughout the length of the English Channel, including the Channel Islands.

In mid-October the winter wrecking season makes a tentative start. Within the next month the number of big predators on the wrecks has grown dramatically and the demand for food is at its greatest. Until spring comes around once more, the offshore angler's life is one of great excitement.

A Porbeagle shark

SAFETY AFLOAT AND ASHORE

Danger can await the unsuspecting angler in the most unlikely and seemingly innocent places. The author remembers walking along a riverbank on a winter's morning, not a high bank but one that appeared very 'safe' and no more than a couple of feet from the water. Without warning, a short section slipped down into the river carrying him with it. His knee-high waders rapidly filled with very cold water and, pushed down by his weight plus that of the tackle-box, rod-holdall and other gear he was carrying, his feet began to sink into the mud that had been formed when the bank collapsed. He was able to scramble out and back on to solid ground, but the danger had been there – the river could have been 7ft (2 m) deep at that spot, or his head could have struck a stone or tree. So, wherever there is water of any amount, there is potential danger and all anglers should be aware of this possibility.

Sea anglers are usually far more safety-conscious than the freshwater sports-man. They are aware that the sea can be calm and placid at one moment and an unforgiving killer the next and every angler going to sea, either in a charter-boat or in his own craft, should have safety as a prime objective, even if he is going no more than 100 yards (91 m) off shore, for it is just as easy to drown in 10 ft (3 m) of water as it is in 50 fathoms.

To be allowed to carry anglers for hire, charterboats must have the appropriate licence and insurance cover and are regularly checked for seaworthiness. They must carry sufficient lifejackets for everyone, the correct signal flares, adequate ship-to-shore radio and also carry radar reflectors. Possibly the most famous last words in sea fishing from boats were: 'That tanker? Oh! He can see us, there's always someone on the lookout!' Don't you believe it: never anchor in a busy sea lane, with or without hoisting the radar reflector.

At sea always have warm clothing as well as waterproofs, even if the weather looks set fair. Other essentials are food and liquid refreshment — preferably non-alcoholic, although there are red-nosed characters who will disagree with the last point and have their own idea about essential supplies. The food should be eaten even if the chances of your suddenly and unpleasantly disposing of it are not unknown, as serious seasickness on an empty stomach can be dangerous. In the author's experience spare food is never wasted and he has enjoyed many an additional snack that the owner has lost interest in!

Never leave sharp bait-cutting knives loose on a gyrating boat — a sudden fall and grab for support can produce a very nasty accident, and you might be fifteen miles (24 km) out in a boat that can only do three knots — work it out!

Never wear smooth-soled wellies when boat fishing or from slippery rocks, especially rocks covered with seaweed. This is not just to avoid falling in, although that in itself can be hazardous, but a wild, gyrating slip from rocks can bring your head into very severe and unrehearsed contact with the rock that your feet left — and the rock will remain undamaged, unlike your head.

Boatfishing in freshwater must be taken seriously where safety is concerned. Some of the large and deep reservoirs are subject to strong winds and it should not be necessary to advise that standing up is not recommended practice. If a change of seat with your fishing partner is needed, move close inshore and do not swap places until you get there.

Fish spines are not usually venomous, the weever being the exception, but sharp spines carry bacteria and will introduce them below the skin if they penetrate it. So take care when handling species such as spurdog, bass, wrasse, perch and so on. However, do not carry out the once prevalent and cruel practice of cutting the spines off the dorsal fins of spurdog before releasing them, for it is a cruel action that removes the fish's defensive and offensive weapons.

Lastly, hooks. The angling cartoon character is often depicted as hooking himself. It might look funny, but take it seriously, for the hook may well carry harmful bacteria on the barb. If you penetrate your skin with a hook, never be brave and try to pull it free as the barb will lacerate the flesh and cause worse wounds. If there are good clean cutting pliers available, snip the shank free, then leave the barb to be removed later by someone medically qualified.

Do's And Don'ts At Sea

ROCK FISHING
Slippery weed-covered rocks are dangerous. To avoid fatal accidents the following rules should be observed.
1. **Never fish alone.**
A companion can go for help should you fall and sprain or break an ankle.
2. **Always watch the rising tide.**
Do not get cut off by an advancing tide.
3. **Always tell someone where you are going** and the estimated time of your return.
4. **Wear suitable footwear.**
Never wear studded waders or smooth-soled wellies on slippery rock faces.

BOAT FISHING
1. **Never fish** in an area without up-to-date sea charts and information about tides.
2. **Be sure** to wear a good quality life-jacket.
3. **Always carry 'in date' flares.** Never use second-hand flares, they may be defective.
4. **At the first sign** of increasing wind strength head for the nearest harbour. Remember that wind and tide together make a calm sea. When the tide changes and comes up against the wind, the surface can change in seconds.
6. **Never** cram too many passengers into a small boat.
7. **If possible** tell someone ashore where you intend to anchor.

Weather Forecasts

An accurate and detailed weather forecast is of vital importance to the saltwater angler, particularly for those who fish afloat. Although a mass of information is readily available from many different creditable sources, it is an unfortunate fact that each year there is an increase in fatalities, especially among anglers operating from small boats. The number of anglers swept from rocks by rough seas also remains unacceptably high. Bad weather is a killer and those who fail to take heed of this fact put their lives, and those of rescuers, at risk.

Rescue services have been called, at great cost to the taxpayer, into action so often that manning levels are being dramatically reduced in an attempt to cut costs. The Coast Guard watch stations, once a familiar feature of prominent headlands around the coast of Britain, have to a large extent been replaced by a mobile Coast Guard. This individual is responsible for such a vast stretch of coastline that, although equipped with improved radio communication with base centres, he is no substitute for a man located high on a clifftop and constantly sweeping his 'patch' with powerful optics. It is a sad fact that should an incident occur on or off a lonely stretch of coast, the chance of rescue is now considerably reduced.

The British Telecom Weatherline Service provides weather forecasts covering much of the British Isles. Areas and telephone numbers are listed in the leading pages of telephone directories. The forecast gives a general condition for a specified area: wind direction and strength, temperatures and an outlook for the next twelve hours, usually timed from 6.00a.m. and 6.00p.m.

Weather Centres, distributed nationwide, can be dialled for a more detailed forecast, but it must be stressed that the workload of meteorologists is such that it is not always possible to get beyond a recorded message. When you are able to get through, precise information is available regarding the existing condition and what it will be in the following twelve hours. The value of this service to charter skippers and boat anglers who need detailed predictions of wind direction and strength, is great. Weather Centres should not be used just to find out if it is going to be sunny or wet. Calls to the service are charged at British Telecom premium rates.

A Weather Consultancy Service is also available at a cost of £30 for a thirty-day period and is on-line around the clock. The subscriber is allotted an ex-directory number which can be dialled from the shore or from a boat at sea, provided the craft has the necessary equipment. The Service is widely used by affluent yachtsmen and calls are received from as far away as the Canary Islands and the Azores. Applications for the Weather Consultancy Service must be made to the Chief Meteorological Officer at one or other of the listed centres.

ABERDEEN (0224) 722334

BRISTOL (0272) 279298

CARDIFF (0222) 397020

GLASGOW (041) 248 3451

MANCHESTER (061) 477 1060

NORWICH (0603) 660779

NEWCASTLE (091) 2326453

SOUTHAMPTON (0703) 228844

MARINE CALL (Tel: 0898 500 458) provides another useful service and gives a detailed forecast of sea conditions, including a five-day forward forecast for the United Kingdom.

Television and radio weather forecasts are based on predictions from the London Weather Centre where Met Officers work with advanced equipment

WEATHER FORECASTS

linked to a variety of weather satellites. The odd hiccup apart, their forecasts are usually extremely accurate. Although the London Centre can be contacted direct, it is better to rely on the regional centre in the area where you are based.

It must, of course, be appreciated that national forecasts, such as those given on television, cover a wide area and local conditions can vary enormously. It is commonsense to always obtain information specifically about the area you are in.

BBC local radio stations provide forecasts, and the times and frequencies are listed in *The Radio Times*. Independent local radio stations also put out forecasts. Local and regional newspapers list the times of broadcast.

National and local newspapers carry a 'Weather Box' and information for specific areas is covered in considerable detail.

Harbour Masters post local forecasts outside their offices and these are particularly useful for information on sea conditions likely to be encountered within five miles (8km) of the port.

Storm cones are flown at principal Coast Guard stations and at most breakwaters and harbours under local council control. When these are up, no craft under 25 ft (22.5 m) should be at sea. A black cone with the point upwards indicates that the wind is coming from a northerly direction and a cone with the point down, from the south.

THE BEAUFORT WIND SCALE

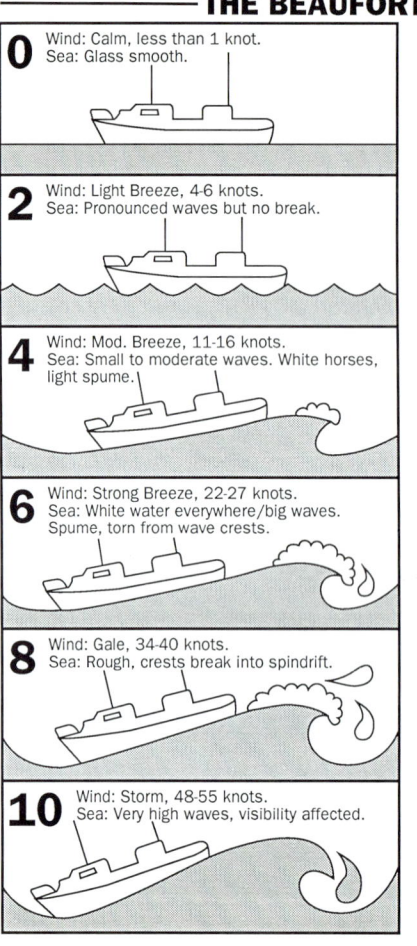

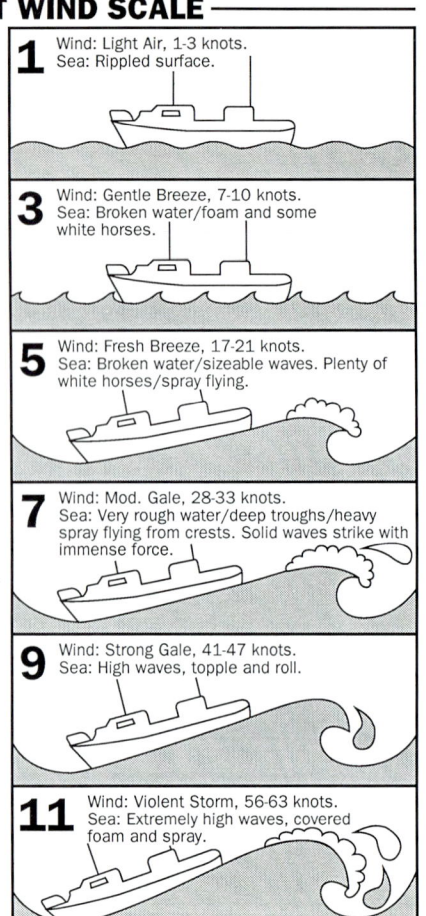

0 Wind: Calm, less than 1 knot.
Sea: Glass smooth.

1 Wind: Light Air, 1-3 knots.
Sea: Rippled surface.

2 Wind: Light Breeze, 4-6 knots.
Sea: Pronounced waves but no break.

3 Wind: Gentle Breeze, 7-10 knots.
Sea: Broken water/foam and some white horses.

4 Wind: Mod. Breeze, 11-16 knots.
Sea: Small to moderate waves. White horses, light spume.

5 Wind: Fresh Breeze, 17-21 knots.
Sea: Broken water/sizeable waves. Plenty of white horses/spray flying.

6 Wind: Strong Breeze, 22-27 knots.
Sea: White water everywhere/big waves. Spume, torn from wave crests.

7 Wind: Mod. Gale, 28-33 knots.
Sea: Very rough water/deep troughs/heavy spray flying from crests. Solid waves strike with immense force.

8 Wind: Gale, 34-40 knots.
Sea: Rough, crests break into spindrift.

9 Wind: Strong Gale, 41-47 knots.
Sea: High waves, topple and roll.

10 Wind: Storm, 48-55 knots.
Sea: Very high waves, visibility affected.

11 Wind: Violent Storm, 56-63 knots.
Sea: Extremely high waves, covered foam and spray.

THE FISHERMAN'S YEARBOOK   WEATHER FORECASTS   111

The Beaufort Wind Scale is closely related to sea conditions.

Sea conditions are influenced by tidal streams. A situation in which there is only a Force 3 wind on the tide can be extremely dangerous for craft up to 20 ft (6 m). Considerable turbulence and backwash can be expected in the vicinity of headlands and rugged coastlines. Sandbars which stretch across many estuaries are dangerous and should be given a wide berth when the sea is rough and the wind is blowing against the direction of the tide. Classic examples are at Padstow and Hayle in Cornwall and Salcombe on the Devon coast.

It is dangerous to go to sea in a small boat without wearing a properly approved life-jacket or a flotation suit or jacket. For the shore angler, a throwing hoop connected to 98 ft (30 m) of light but strong, nylon rope should be as much a part of the day's equipment as the rod and reel. It is also wise to carry a pack of flares. Most chandlers and marine centres sell a variety of types which are highly effective and competitively priced.

Mike Millman

NAUTICAL MEASURES
6 feet = 1 fathom
100 fathoms = 1 cable
10 cables = 1 nautical mile
1 nautical mile = 6080 feet or 1.151 statute miles
3 miles = 1 league

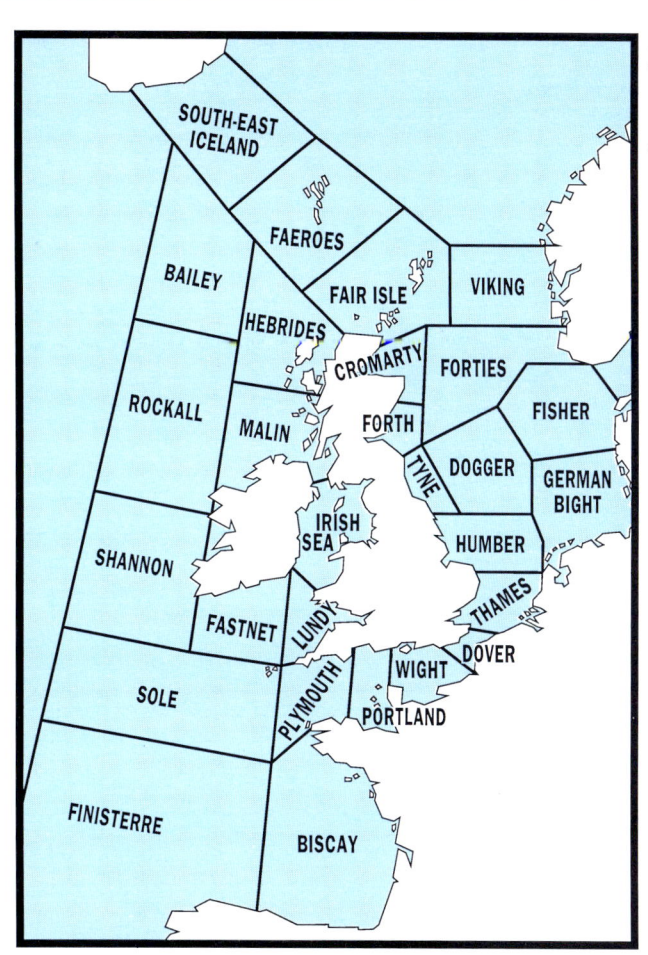

SHIPPING WEATHER FORECAST AREAS

VISIBILITY SCALE

Description	Limit of visibility
0 Dense fog	50 yds
1 Thick fog	300 yds
2 Fog	600 yds
3 Moderate fog	½ mile
4 Mist or thin fog	1 mile
5 Poor visibility	2 miles
6 Moderate visibility	5 miles
7 Good visibility	10 miles
8 Very good visibility	30 miles
9 Exceptional visibility	over 30 miles

Time zone G.M.T.　　　　　　　　　　　　　　　　TIDAL PREDICTIONS OF HIGH WATERS　　　　　　　　　　　　　　　　Units　Metres
DATUM OF PREDICTIONS = CHART DATUM : 3.20 METRES BELOW ORDNANCE DATUM (NEWLYN)

LONDON BRIDGE — January 1989

Day		Day	MORN. H.	MORN. M.	HT. M.	AFT. H.	AFT. M.	HT. M.
1	SU		07	30	5.6	20	15	5.7
2	M		08	34	5.5	21	14	5.7
3	TU		09	38	5.5	22	13	5.8
4	W		10	38	5.7	23	09	6.0
5	TH		11	37	5.9	**	**	***
6	F		00	07	6.2	12	35	6.2
7	SA		01	02	6.5	13	28	6.6
8	SU		01	51	6.8	14	16	6.9
9	M		02	36	7.0	15	03	7.2
10	TU		03	18	7.1	15	46	7.4
11	W		04	00	7.2	16	30	7.3
12	TH		04	41	7.1	17	15	7.1
13	F		05	22	6.9	18	01	6.8
14	SA		06	07	6.7	18	52	6.5
15	SU		06	56	6.5	19	49	6.3
16	M		07	58	6.4	20	57	6.2
17	TU		09	12	6.2	22	09	6.2
18	W		10	34	6.1	23	20	6.2
19	TH		11	51	6.2	**	**	***
20	F		00	25	6.3	12	52	6.4
21	SA		01	17	6.4	13	42	6.5
22	SU		02	01	6.5	14	25	6.7
23	M		02	40	6.7	15	04	6.9
24	TU		03	15	6.8	15	39	7.0
25	W		03	49	6.8	16	13	6.9
26	TH		04	20	6.8	16	45	6.8
27	F		04	51	6.6	17	18	6.6
28	SA		05	22	6.4	17	51	6.4
29	SU		05	57	6.2	18	28	6.1
30	M		06	35	5.9	19	10	5.9
31	TU		07	21	5.5	20	04	5.6

LONDON BRIDGE — February 1989

Day		MORN. H.	MORN. M.	HT. M.	AFT. H.	AFT. M.	HT. M.
1	W	08	29	5.3	21	11	5.5
2	TH	09	46	5.4	22	23	5.6
3	F	11	02	5.6	23	37	5.9
4	SA	**	**	***	12	17	6.1
5	SU	00	43	6.4	13	14	6.7
6	M	01	35	6.8	14	04	7.2
7	TU	02	20	7.2	14	49	7.5
8	W	03	03	7.4	15	31	7.6
9	TH	03	42	7.5	16	13	7.6
10	F	04	21	7.4	16	55	7.3
11	SA	05	02	7.2	17	37	6.9
12	SU	05	43	7.0	18	22	6.5
13	M	06	29	6.6	19	13	6.2
14	TU	07	27	6.3	20	15	6.0
15	W	08	42	6.0	21	29	5.8
16	TH	10	12	5.9	22	57	5.9
17	F	11	39	6.1	**	**	***
18	SA	00	08	6.2	12	41	6.4
19	SU	01	02	6.4	13	28	6.7
20	M	01	45	6.6	14	09	6.9
21	TU	02	22	6.8	14	44	7.0
22	W	02	54	6.9	15	17	7.0
23	TH	03	24	6.9	15	45	7.0
24	F	03	52	6.9	16	13	6.9
25	SA	04	20	6.8	16	42	6.8
26	SU	04	49	6.6	17	13	6.6
27	M	05	22	6.4	17	46	6.4
28	TU	05	58	6.1	18	24	6.1

LONDON BRIDGE — March 1989

Day		MORN. H.	MORN. M.	HT. M.	AFT. H.	AFT. M.	HT. M.
1	W	06	41	5.7	19	09	5.6
2	TH	07	40	5.4	20	13	5.4
3	F	09	03	5.3	21	41	5.4
4	SA	10	37	5.6	23	12	5.8
5	SU	11	57	6.2	**	**	***
6	M	00	21	6.4	12	55	6.9
7	TU	01	13	6.9	13	42	7.4
8	W	01	58	7.3	14	27	7.6
9	TH	02	39	7.6	15	08	7.7
10	F	03	18	7.7	15	50	7.6
11	SA	03	59	7.6	16	31	7.3
12	SU	04	40	7.4	17	12	6.9
13	M	05	22	7.0	17	54	6.5
14	TU	06	10	6.6	18	41	6.1
15	W	07	06	6.2	19	38	5.8
16	TH	08	18	5.9	20	51	5.6
17	F	09	48	5.8	22	27	5.7
18	SA	11	18	6.1	23	44	6.1
19	SU	**	**	***	12	19	6.6
20	M	00	38	6.5	13	06	6.9
21	TU	01	20	6.7	13	45	7.0
22	W	01	57	6.9	14	19	7.0
23	TH	02	27	6.9	14	47	7.0
24	F	02	56	6.9	15	14	6.9
25	SA	03	21	6.9	15	39	6.9
26	SU	03	49	6.8	16	07	6.9
27	M	04	21	6.7	16	40	6.8
28	TU	04	55	6.5	17	12	6.6
29	W	05	33	6.3	17	50	6.2
30	TH	06	18	6.0	18	36	5.9
31	F	07	16	5.6	19	38	5.5

TIDAL PREDICTIONS OF HIGH WATERS
Time zone G.M.T. DATUM OF PREDICTIONS = CHART DATUM : 3.20 METRES BELOW ORDNANCE DATUM (NEWLYN) Units Metres

LONDON BRIDGE — April 1989

		MORN. H.	M.	HT. M.	AFT. H.	M.	HT. M.
1	SA	08	39	5.5	21	07	5.5
2	SU	10	14	5.8	22	42	5.8
3	M	11	32	6.4	23	53	6.4
4	TU	**	**	***	12	31	7.0
5	W	00	46	6.0	13	19	7.4
6	TH	01	31	7.3	14	02	7.5
7	F	02	13	7.5	14	44	7.5
8	SA	02	54	7.6	15	25	7.4
9	SU	03	36	7.6	16	06	7.2
10	M	04	20	7.4	16	48	6.9
11	TU	05	06	7.0	17	30	6.5
12	W	05	56	6.6	18	15	6.1
13	TH	06	50	6.2	19	10	5.8
14	F	07	57	5.9	20	18	5.5
15	SA	09	15	5.7	21	43	5.5
16	SU	10	44	6.0	23	09	5.9
17	M	11	47	6.4	**	**	***
18	TU	00	05	6.4	12	35	6.8
19	W	00	49	6.7	13	13	6.9
20	TH	01	26	6.8	13	47	6.9
21	F	01	57	6.8	14	15	6.9
22	SA	02	23	6.8	14	40	6.9
23	SU	02	53	6.8	15	08	6.9
24	M	03	24	6.8	15	39	6.9
25	TU	03	59	6.7	16	13	6.8
26	W	04	35	6.6	16	49	6.6
27	TH	05	18	6.5	17	29	6.4
28	F	06	07	6.2	18	17	6.0
29	SA	07	06	6.0	19	20	5.8
20	SU	08	23	5.9	20	43	5.7

LONDON BRIDGE — May 1989

		MORN. H.	M.	HT. M.	AFT. H.	M.	HT. M.
1	M	09	48	6.1	22	09	6.0
2	TU	11	02	6.6	23	19	6.5
3	W	**	**	***	12	03	7.0
4	TH	00	15	6.9	12	53	7.2
5	F	01	04	7.1	13	38	7.2
6	SA	01	49	7.2	14	22	7.2
7	SU	02	33	7.3	15	03	7.1
8	M	03	19	7.3	15	46	7.0
9	TU	04	06	7.2	16	30	6.8
10	W	04	54	7.0	17	12	6.5
11	TH	05	43	6.6	17	56	6.1
12	F	06	34	6.3	18	45	5.8
13	SA	07	30	6.0	19	44	5.6
14	SU	08	34	5.8	20	54	5.6
15	M	09	50	5.9	22	14	5.7
16	TU	11	01	6.1	23	20	6.1
17	W	11	53	6.4	**	**	***
18	TH	00	08	6.3	12	34	6.6
19	F	00	48	6.5	13	07	6.6
20	SA	01	21	6.5	13	40	6.7
21	SU	01	54	6.6	14	11	6.7
22	M	02	29	6.6	14	46	6.8
23	TU	03	07	6.7	15	21	6.8
24	W	03	46	6.8	15	59	6.8
25	TH	04	27	6.8	16	38	6.7
26	F	05	12	6.7	17	20	6.5
27	SA	06	00	6.5	18	08	6.3
28	SU	06	57	6.3	19	04	6.1
29	M	08	04	6.2	20	16	6.1
30	TU	09	19	6.3	21	32	6.3
31	W	10	30	6.6	22	44	6.5

LONDON BRIDGE — June 1989

		MORN. H.	M.	HT. M.	AFT. H.	M.	HT. M.
1	TH	11	33	6.7	23	47	6.6
2	F	**	**	***	12	29	6.8
3	SA	00	42	6.7	13	19	6.7
4	SU	01	33	6.7	14	04	6.7
5	M	02	22	6.9	14	47	6.8
6	TU	03	10	7.0	15	31	6.8
7	W	03	56	7.1	16	14	6.8
8	TH	04	41	7.0	16	55	6.6
9	F	05	26	6.8	17	36	6.3
10	SA	06	10	6.4	18	18	6.1
11	SU	06	57	6.2	19	06	5.9
12	M	07	49	5.9	20	05	5.7
13	TU	08	50	5.8	21	11	5.7
14	W	09	52	5.8	22	16	5.8
15	TH	10	51	6.0	23	13	5.9
16	F	11	40	6.1	**	**	***
17	SA	00	03	6.1	12	24	6.3
18	SU	00	46	6.2	13	07	6.5
19	M	01	30	6.4	13	49	6.6
20	TU	02	13	6.6	14	32	6.7
21	W	02	57	6.8	15	12	6.8
22	TH	03	39	6.9	15	53	6.8
23	F	04	21	7.0	16	33	6.8
24	SA	05	05	6.9	17	12	6.7
25	SU	05	50	6.7	17	56	6.6
26	M	06	41	6.5	18	45	6.5
27	TU	07	38	6.4	19	45	6.4
28	W	08	46	6.3	20	57	6.3
29	TH	09	56	6.4	22	12	6.3
30	F	11	05	6.4	23	25	6.3

Time zone G.M.T.　　　　　　　　　　　　　TIDAL PREDICTIONS OF HIGH WATERS　　　　　　　　　　　　　Units　Metres
DATUM OF PREDICTIONS = CHART DATUM : 3.20 METRES BELOW ORDNANCE DATUM (NEWLYN)

LONDON BRIDGE — July 1989

		MORN. H.	M.	HT. M.	AFT. H.	M.	HT. M.
1	SA	**	**	***	12	08	6.4
2	SU	00	31	6.4	13	04	6.4
3	M	01	27	6.4	13	54	6.4
4	TU	02	16	6.6	14	37	6.6
5	W	03	01	6.8	15	18	6.7
6	TH	03	43	7.0	15	57	6.8
7	F	04	24	7.0	16	34	6.7
8	SA	05	02	6.8	17	11	6.6
9	SU	05	40	6.6	17	46	6.4
10	M	06	18	6.3	18	25	6.1
11	TU	07	02	6.1	19	13	5.9
12	W	07	52	5.8	20	12	5.6
13	TH	08	49	5.7	21	14	5.5
14	F	09	46	5.7	22	14	5.5
15	SA	10	44	5.8	23	16	5.7
16	SU	11	43	6.0	**	**	***
17	M	00	18	5.9	12	42	6.2
18	TU	01	12	6.3	13	33	6.5
19	W	02	01	6.7	14	19	6.8
20	TH	02	44	7.0	15	01	7.0
21	F	03	28	7.2	15	41	7.1
22	SA	04	09	7.3	16	19	7.1
23	SU	04	49	7.1	16	57	7.0
24	M	05	32	6.9	17	36	6.8
25	TU	06	17	6.6	18	21	6.7
26	W	07	09	6.3	19	14	6.4
27	TH	08	11	6.1	20	25	6.2
28	F	09	22	6.1	21	46	6.1
29	SA	10	40	6.1	23	12	6.1
30	SU	11	53	6.2	**	**	***
31	M	00	24	6.3	12	53	6.3

LONDON BRIDGE — August 1989

		MORN. H.	M.	HT. M.	AFT. H.	M.	HT. M.
1	TU	01	21	6.5	13	42	6.5
2	W	02	08	6.7	14	25	6.6
3	TH	02	49	6.9	15	01	6.8
4	F	03	25	7.0	15	36	6.9
5	SA	04	00	7.0	16	09	6.8
6	SU	04	33	6.9	16	40	6.7
7	M	05	05	6.7	17	11	6.6
8	TU	05	37	6.5	17	46	6.3
9	W	06	12	6.2	18	25	6.0
10	TH	06	55	5.9	19	12	5.6
11	F	07	44	5.6	20	12	5.3
12	SA	08	46	5.4	21	24	5.3
13	SU	09	55	5.4	22	38	5.4
14	M	11	11	5.7	23	56	5.9
15	TU	**	**	***	12	21	6.1
16	W	00	53	6.4	13	14	6.6
17	TH	01	42	7.0	13	59	7.0
18	F	02	26	7.3	14	40	7.3
19	SA	03	07	7.5	15	18	7.5
20	SU	03	48	7.5	15	56	7.5
21	M	04	28	7.3	16	34	7.3
22	TU	05	09	6.9	17	15	7.0
23	W	05	51	6.5	17	58	6.7
24	TH	06	39	6.2	18	53	6.4
25	F	07	38	5.9	20	05	6.1
26	SA	08	51	5.8	21	29	5.9
27	SU	10	16	5.8	23	01	6.1
28	M	11	36	1.1	**	**	***
29	TU	00	12	6.5	12	38	6.5
30	W	01	07	6.8	13	26	6.7
31	TH	01	51	7.0	14	0.5	6.9

LONDON BRIDGE — September 1989

		MORN. H.	M.	HT. M.	AFT. H.	M.	HT. M.
1	F	02	29	7.0	14	40	6.9
2	SA	03	01	7.0	15	11	7.0
3	SU	03	32	6.9	15	39	6.9
4	M	03	59	6.8	16	06	6.8
5	TU	04	27	6.7	16	35	6.7
6	W	04	57	6.6	17	09	6.5
7	TH	05	30	6.4	17	46	6.1
8	F	06	07	6.1	18	29	5.8
9	SA	06	50	5.7	19	23	5.4
10	SU	07	48	5.4	20	37	5.2
11	M	09	08	5.3	22	09	5.4
12	TU	10	42	5.6	23	32	6.0
13	W	11	56	6.2	**	**	***
14	TH	00	29	6.7	12	48	6.8
15	F	01	17	7.2	13	33	7.2
16	SA	02	01	7.5	14	13	7.5
17	SU	02	43	7.6	14	51	7.7
18	M	03	22	7.5	15	31	7.7
19	TU	04	03	7.3	16	13	7.5
20	W	04	44	6.9	16	57	7.1
21	TH	05	27	6.5	17	44	6.7
22	F	06	15	6.1	18	41	6.3
23	SA	07	13	5.8	19	51	5.9
24	SU	08	23	5.6	21	11	5.8
25	M	09	49	5.7	22	42	6.1
26	TU	11	13	6.1	23	53	6.6
27	W	**	**	***	12	14	6.6
28	TH	00	43	7.0	13	00	6.9
29	F	01	26	7.1	13	40	7.0
30	SA	02	02	7.1	14	12	7.0

Time zone G.M.T.
TIDAL PREDICTIONS OF HIGH WATERS
DATUM OF PREDICTIONS = CHART DATUM : 3.20 METRES BELOW ORDNANCE DATUM (NEWLYN)
Units Metres

LONDON BRIDGE — October 1989

Day		MORN. H.	M.	HT. M.	AFT. H.	M.	HT. M.
1	SU	02	33	7.0	14	42	7.0
2	M	03	00	6.9	15	07	6.9
3	TU	03	24	6.9	15	35	6.8
4	W	03	50	6.8	16	06	6.7
5	TH	04	21	6.7	16	40	6.6
6	F	04	55	6.5	17	18	6.3
7	SA	05	32	6.2	18	01	6.0
8	SU	06	15	5.9	18	55	5.7
9	M	07	12	5.5	20	06	5.5
10	TU	08	32	5.4	21	39	5.6
11	W	10	09	5.7	23	01	6.2
12	TH	11	22	6.3	**	**	***
13	F	00	01	6.8	12	17	6.9
14	SA	00	50	7.2	13	03	7.3
15	SU	01	34	7.4	13	45	7.5
16	M	02	16	7.5	14	26	7.7
17	TU	02	57	7.4	15	08	7.7
18	W	03	39	7.2	15	55	7.5
19	TH	04	24	6.9	16	42	7.2
20	F	05	09	6.5	17	34	6.7
21	SA	05	57	6.1	18	31	6.3
22	SU	06	52	5.8	19	34	6.0
23	M	07	57	5.6	20	46	5.8
24	TU	09	14	5.6	22	10	6.0
25	W	10	40	5.9	23	22	6.4
26	TH	11	43	6.4	**	**	***
27	F	00	14	6.8	12	29	6.8
28	SA	00	56	7.0	13	09	7.0
29	SU	01	31	7.0	13	42	7.0
30	M	02	01	6.9	14	11	6.9
31	TU	02	26	6.9	14	39	6.9

LONDON BRIDGE — November 1989

Day		MORN. H.	M.	HT. M.	AFT. H.	M.	HT. M.
1	W	02	53	6.9	15	19	6.8
2	TH	03	22	6.8	15	43	6.7
3	F	03	55	6.7	16	20	6.6
4	SA	04	31	6.6	16	59	6.5
5	SU	05	09	6.4	17	44	6.3
6	M	05	53	6.1	18	38	6.0
7	TU	06	48	5.8	19	45	5.8
8	W	08	01	5.7	21	08	5.9
9	TH	09	29	5.9	22	26	6.3
10	F	10	44	6.3	23	29	6.8
11	SA	11	43	6.8	**	**	***
12	SU	00	22	7.1	12	35	7.1
13	M	01	10	7.1	13	21	7.2
14	TU	01	54	7.1	14	06	7.3
15	W	02	37	7.1	14	54	7.4
16	TH	03	22	7.0	15	43	7.4
17	F	04	07	6.9	16	34	7.2
18	SA	04	54	6.6	17	25	6.9
19	SU	05	42	6.3	18	15	6.5
20	M	06	29	6.0	19	10	6.1
21	TU	07	24	5.8	20	11	5.9
22	W	08	29	5.7	21	21	5.9
23	TH	09	48	5.8	22	35	6.1
24	F	10	59	6.1	23	33	6.4
25	SA	11	53	6.4	**	**	***
26	SU	00	18	6.6	12	35	6.6
27	M	00	55	6.7	13	10	6.7
28	TU	01	27	6.7	13	44	6.7
29	W	01	58	6.8	14	16	6.7
30	TH	02	30	6.8	14	53	6.7

LONDON BRIDGE — December 1989

Day		MORN. H.	M.	HT. M.	AFT. H.	M.	HT. M.
1	F	03	05	6.8	15	31	6.8
2	SA	03	42	6.8	16	10	6.8
3	SU	04	19	6.7	16	51	6.7
4	M	04	58	6.5	17	34	6.5
5	TU	05	40	6.4	18	24	6.3
6	W	06	28	6.2	19	23	6.1
7	TH	07	30	6.1	20	34	6.1
8	F	08	47	6.1	21	49	6.3
9	SA	10	04	6.3	22	58	6.6
10	SU	11	12	6.6	23	57	6.7
11	M	**	**	***	12	12	6.7
12	TU	00	50	6.8	13	07	6.8
13	W	01	40	6.7	13	58	6.9
14	TH	02	26	6.8	14	47	7.1
15	F	03	11	6.9	15	36	7.2
16	SA	03	56	6.9	16	23	7.2
17	SU	04	38	6.8	17	08	7.0
18	M	05	20	6.6	17	53	6.7
19	TU	06	03	6.3	18	38	6.3
20	W	06	48	6.0	19	28	6.0
21	TH	07	41	5.8	20	25	5.8
22	F	08	46	5.7	21	28	5.8
23	SA	09	55	5.7	22	33	5.9
24	SU	11	01	5.9	23	29	6.1
25	M	11	54	6.0	**	**	***
26	TU	00	15	6.3	12	39	6.2
27	W	00	56	6.5	13	21	6.4
28	TH	01	37	6.6	14	02	6.6
29	F	02	18	6.8	14	43	6.8
30	SA	02	57	6.9	15	24	7.0
31	SU	03	35	6.9	16	03	7.0

Copyright Reserved. Tidal predictions by Tidal Computation and Statistics Section, Proudman Oceanographic Laboratory, Bidston Observatory, Birkenhead, Merseyside, UK.

WEATHER FORECASTS

The following time differences will, when applied to the standard port, give the approximate time of high water at the port designated. Resultant times will be in the time zone of the basic tide table.

Standard Port: LONDON BRIDGE

Secondary Port:-	Hr	Min
ABERDEEN	-0	21
ABERYSTWYTH	-6	09
ARRAN (LAMLASH)	-1	54
AYR	-1	53
BANFF	-1	46
BARMOUTH	-5	36
BARROW-IN-FURNESS	-2	24
BELFAST	-2	45
BERWICK-ON-TWEED	+0	56
BIDEFORD	+4	17
BLACKPOOL	-2	49
BOGNOR REGIS	-2	41
BOURNEMOUTH	-5	03*
BRIDLINGTON	+3	01
BRIGHTON	-2	50
BUDE HAVEN	+3	59
CAERNARVON	-3	57
CARDIFF (PENARTH)	+5	17
CLACTON-ON-SEA	-1	59
COWES	-2	23
CROMER	+5	00
DARTMOUTH	+4	37
DEAL	-2	37
DOUGLAS (ISLE OF MAN)	-2	43
DOVER	-2	52
DUNDEE	+1	09
DUNGENESS	-3	04
EASTBOURNE	-2	50
EXMOUTH DOCK	+4	55
FALMOUTH	+3	35
FELIXSTOWE	-2	16
FILEY BAY	+2	48
FISHGUARD	+5	46
FOLKESTONE	-3	04
FOWEY	+3	53
GAIRLOCH	+5	16
GARLIESTON	-2	09
GIRVAN	-2	00
GORLESTON	-5	00
GRIMSBY	+4	13
HARTLEPOOL	+1	56
HARWICH	-2	02
HASTINGS	-2	57
HERNE BAY	-1	24
HOLYHEAD	-3	27
ILFRACOMBE	+4	22
INVERNESS	-1	37
IRVINE	-1	48
KING'S LYNN	+4	50
KYLE OF LOCHALSH	+5	06
LEITH	+0	58
LITTLEHAMPTON (ENTRANCE)	-2	38
LLANDUDNO	-3	09
LONDONDERRY	-5	37
LOOE	+3	55
LOWESTOFT	-4	25
LOSSIEMOUTH	-2	03
LYME REGIS	+4	55
MARGATE	-1	52
MENAI BRIDGE	-3	07
MILFORD HAVEN	+4	39
MONTROSE	+0	39
MORECAMBE	-2	32
NEWLYN	+3	08
NEWQUAY	+3	34
OBAN	+4	17
ORFORDNESS	-2	50
PEEL (ISLE OF MAN)	-1	41
PENZANCE (SEE NEWLYN)		
PETERHEAD	-1	01
PLYMOUTH	+4	05
PORTHCAWL	+4	39
PORTLAND	+5	10
PORTSMOUTH	-2	23
PWLLHELI	-5	46
RAMSEY (ISLE OF MAN)	-2	35
RAMSGATE	-2	32
SALCOMBE	+4	10
SCARBOROUGH	+2	31
SKEGNESS	+4	32
SOUTHEND	-1	22
SOUTHPORT	-2	54
SOUTHSEA (SEE PORTSMOUTH)		
SOUTH SHIELDS (SEE TYNEMOUTH)		
SOUTHWOLD	-3	50
SUNDERLAND	+1	49
SWANAGE	-5	13*
SWANSEA	+4	43
TEIGNMOUTH (APPROACHES)	+4	37
TENBY	+4	27
TORQUAY	+4	40
TYNEMOUTH	+1	54
VENTNOR	-2	50
WESTON-SUPER-MARE	+5	07
WHITBY	+2	20
WHITEHAVEN	-2	29
WIGTOWN BAY (SEE GARLIESTON)		
WICK	-2	28
YARMOUTH (ISLE OF WIGHT)	-3	28*

*1st high water springs

DIARY FOR 1989

PHASES OF THE MOON

	New Moon date	New Moon time		First Quarter date	First Quarter time		Full Moon date	Full Moon time		Last Quarter date	Last Quarter time
Jan.	7	19.22	Jan.	14	13.58	Jan.	21	21.33	Jan	30	02.02
Feb.	6	07.37	Feb.	12	23.15	Feb.	20	15.32	Feb.	28	20.08
Mar.	7	18.19	Mar.	14	10.11	Mar.	22	09.58	Mar.	30	10.21
Apr.	6	03.33	Apr.	12	23.13	Apr.	21	03.13	Apr.	28	20.46
May	5	11.46	May	12	14.19	May	20	18.16	May	28	04.01
June	3	19.53	June	11	06.59	June	19	06.57	June	26	09.09
July	3	04.59	July	11	00.19	July	18	17.42	July	25	13.31
Aug.	1	16.06	Aug.	9	17.28	Aug.	17	03.07	Aug.	23	18.40
Aug.	31	05.44	Sept.	8	09.49	Sept.	15	11.51	Sept.	22	02.10
Sept.	29	21.47	Oct.	8	00.52	Oct.	14	20.32	Oct.	21	13.19
Oct.	29	15.27	Nov.	6	14.11	Nov.	13	05.51	Nov.	20	04.44
Nov.	28	09.41	Dec.	6	01.26	Dec.	12	16.30	Dec.	19	23.54
Dec.	28	03.20									

Reproduced, with permission, from data supplied by the Science and Engineering Research Council. The Science and Engineering Research Council does not accept any responsibility for loss or damage arising from the use of information contained in any of its reports or in any communication about its tests or investigations.

Holidays for 1989

The following list contains bank holidays, common law holidays and days to be given in lieu for holidays which fall on a weekend. There is no statutory requirement for a day to be given in lieu if one of the additional holidays falls on a Sunday or if any holiday falls on a Saturday, but the probable dates of days 'to be given in lieu' which have not yet been authorised by Royal proclamation are given in parentheses.

In Scotland and Nothern Ireland a general holiday is not necessarily observed on the same day as the bank holiday.

1989	England & Wales	Northern Ireland	Scotland
New Year	Jan 1⁄, (Jan 2)	Jan 1⁄, (Jan 2)	Jan 2, Jan 3
St Patrick	—	Mar. 17	—
Good Friday	Mar 24≠	Mar 24≠	Mar 24
Easter Monday	Mar 27	Mar 27	—
May Day	May 1	May 1	May 29
Spring	May 29	May 29	May 1
Battle of the Boyne	—	July 12	—
Summer	Aug 28	Aug 28	Aug 7
Christmas	Dec 25≠ Dec 26	Dec 25≠ Dec 26	Dec 25≠ Dec 26

≠Common Law Holiday * Holiday falls on a Saturday
⁄ Holiday falls on a Sunday

JANUARY

SUN 1	SUN 8
MON 2	MON 9
TUE 3	TUE 10
WED 4	WED 11
THU 5	THU 12
FRI 6	FRI 13
SAT 7	SAT 14

JANUARY

SUN **15**	**SUN** **22**
MON **16**	**MON** **23**
TUE **17**	**TUE** **24**
WED **18**	**WED** **25**
THU **19**	**THU** **26**
FRI **20**	**FRI** **27**
SAT **21**	**SAT** **28**

JANUARY/FEBRUARY

SUN
29

MON
30

TUE
31

WED
1

THU
2

FRI
3

SAT
4

SUN
5

MON
6

TUE
7

WED
8

THU
9

FRI
10

SAT
11

FEBRUARY

SUN
12

MON
13

TUE
14

WED
15

THU
16

FRI
17

SAT
18

SUN
19

MON
20

TUE
21

WED
22

THU
23

FRI
24

SAT
25

FEBRUARY/MARCH

SUN **26**	**SUN** **5**
MON **27**	**MON** **6**
TUE **28**	**TUE** **7**
WED **1**	**WED** **8**
THU **2**	**THU** **9**
FRI **3**	**FRI** **10**
SAT **4**	**SAT** **11**

MARCH

SUN
12

MON
13

TUE
14

WED
15

THU
16

FRI
17

SAT
18

SUN
19

MON
20

TUE
21

WED
22

THU
23

FRI
24

SAT
25

MARCH/APRIL

SUN
26

MON
27

TUE
28

WED
29

THU
30

FRI
31

SAT
1

SUN
2

MON
3

TUE
4

WED
5

THU
6

FRI
7

SAT
8

THE FISHERMAN'S YEARBOOK   APRIL   **125**

SUN
9

SUN
16

MON
10

MON
17

TUE
11

TUE
18

WED
12

WED
19

THU
13

THU
20

FRI
14

FRI
21

SAT
15

SAT
22

APRIL/MAY

SUN
23

MON
24

TUE
25

WED
26

THU
27

FRI
28

SAT
29

SUN
30

MON
1

TUE
2

WED
3

THU
4

FRI
5

SAT
6

MAY

SUN
7

MON
8

TUE
9

WED
10

THU
11

FRI
12

SAT
13

SUN
14

MON
15

TUE
16

WED
17

THU
18

FRI
19

SAT
20

MAY/JUNE

SUN *21*	**SUN** *28*
MON *22*	**MON** *29*
TUE *23*	**TUE** *30*
WED *24*	**WED** *31*
THU *25*	**THU** *1*
FRI *26*	**FRI** *2*
SAT *27*	**SAT** *3*

JUNE

SUN
4

MON
5

TUE
6

WED
7

THU
8

FRI
9

SAT
10

SUN
11

MON
12

TUE
13

WED
14

THU
15

FRI
16

SAT
17

JUNE/JULY

SUN
18

MON
19

TUE
20

WED
21

THU
22

FRI
23

SAT
24

SUN
25

MON
26

TUE
27

WED
28

THU
29

FRI
30

SAT
1

JULY

SUN
2

MON
3

TUE
4

WED
5

THU
6

FRI
7

SAT
8

SUN
9

MON
10

TUE
11

WED
12

THU
13

FRI
14

SAT
15

JULY

SUN
16

SUN
23

MON
17

MON
24

TUE
18

TUE
25

WED
19

WED
26

THU
20

THU
27

FRI
21

FRI
28

SAT
22

SAT
29

JULY/AUGUST

SUN
30

MON
31

TUE
1

WED
2

THU
3

FRI
4

SAT
5

SUN
6

MON
7

TUE
8

WED
9

THU
10

FRI
11

SAT
12

AUGUST

SUN
13

MON
14

TUE
15

WED
16

THU
17

FRI
18

SAT
19

SUN
20

MON
21

TUE
22

WED
23

THU
24

FRI
25

SAT
26

AUGUST/SEPTEMBER

SUN
27

MON
28

TUE
29

WED
30

THU
31

FRI
1

SAT
2

SUN
3

MON
4

TUE
5

WED
6

THU
7

FRI
8

SAT
9

SEPTEMBER

SUN **10**	**SUN** **17**
MON **11**	**MON** **18**
TUE **12**	**TUE** **19**
WED **13**	**WED** **20**
THU **14**	**THU** **21**
FRI **15**	**FRI** **22**
SAT **16**	**SAT** **23**

SEPTEMBER/OCTOBER

SUN 24	**SUN** 1
MON 25	**MON** 2
TUE 26	**TUE** 3
WED 27	**WED** 4
THU 28	**THU** 5
FRI 29	**FRI** 6
SAT 30	**SAT** 7

OCTOBER

SUN
8

MON
9

TUE
10

WED
11

THU
12

FRI
13

SAT
14

SUN
15

MON
16

TUE
17

WED
18

THU
19

FRI
20

SAT
21

THE FISHERMAN'S YEARBOOK

OCTOBER/NOVEMBER

SUN 22	**SUN** 29
MON 23	**MON** 30
TUE 24	**TUE** 31
WED 25	**WED** 1
THU 26	**THU** 2
FRI 27	**FRI** 3
SAT 28	**SAT** 4

NOVEMBER

SUN
5

SUN
12

MON
6

MON
13

TUE
7

TUE
14

WED
8

WED
15

THU
9

THU
16

FRI
10

FRI
17

SAT
11

SAT
18

THE FISHERMAN'S YEARBOOK — NOVEMBER/DECEMBER

SUN
19

MON
20

TUE
21

WED
22

THU
23

FRI
24

SAT
25

SUN
26

MON
27

TUE
28

WED
29

THU
30

FRI
1

SAT
2

DECEMBER

SUN
3

SUN
10

MON
4

MON
11

TUE
5

TUE
12

WED
6

WED
13

THU
7

THU
14

FRI
8

FRI
15

SAT
9

SAT
16

DECEMBER

SUN 17

MON 18

TUE 19

WED 20

THU 21

FRI 22

SAT 23

SUN 24

MON 25

TUE 26

WED 27

THU 28

FRI 29

SAT/SUN 30/31

THE CONTRIBUTORS

JOHN BAILEY is one of the country's leading specialist anglers. His list of specimen catches include carp and pike to over 30 lb, roach to 31 lb 10 oz, barbel and bream in double figures, perch to 31 lb 12 oz, chub to 51 lb 15 oz and rudd to over 31 lb. As an angling journalist he has contributed to *Anglers' Mail, Coarse Fisherman* and other angling publications. His books include *In Visible Waters* (1984), *Tracks with a Two Piece* (1985) and with Martyn Page co-author of *Pike – The Predator Becomes the Prey* and *Carp – The Quest for the Queen.*

LEN CACUTT was the founding editor of the *Anglers' Mail* and editor of *The Fisherman's Handbook*. He has contributed to numerous angling books and publications and edited the Collins' *Pocket Book Guides to Angling.* Among his published works are *The Angling Club Handbook, British Freshwater Fishes* and most recently, the Guinness Book of *Angling Records.*

TREVOR HOUSBY Author, photographer, travel writer and angling consultant, Trevor Housby, in addition to being one of Britain's foremost sea and game anglers, finds relaxation in fishing for big game all over the world. Among the twenty-two books he has published in the UK, Italy, Spain and Switzerland are *Whaling in the Azores, Shark Fishing, Freshwater Fishing, Trout Fishing, Big Game Fishing,* and, most recently, *Specimen Hunter.* He is a regular contributor to the international angling press and is angling advisor to the governments of Bermuda and the Azores.

MIKE MILLMAN, angling writer and photographer, is a major contributor to leading angling publications in Britain, Germany and Scandinavia. A well-known sea angler, he has fished all over the world and is saltwater angling consultant to the Shakespeare Company. A former England International, he has won many top competitions including the British Conger Championship. In addition to his writing and fishing, he is president of a number of angling clubs and chairman of the South West Federation of Sea Anglers.

KEN WHITEHEAD is essentially a pike angler (his best fish weighing well over 30 lb) but he is also a keen game fisherman and regularly fishes for sewin and salmon in Wales and for coarse fish throughout his native Sussex. He is a lone angler who fishes for pleasure, is wary of angling politics and distrustful of complicated fishing tackle and garrulous anglers. His book *Pike Fishing* was published by David & Charles in 1987.

JOHN WILSON, apart from his career as coarse angler, author, journalist, photographer and TV presenter, has run a tackle shop in Norwich since 1971. His specimen catches include a 6 lb 7 oz chub, 1 lb 1 oz dace, 7 lb 1½ oz tench and 11 lb 3 oz zander. A regular contributor to British, German and American angling magazines, his books include *Where to Fish in Norfolk and Suffolk* and *A Specimen Fishing Year.* He has recently become known to millions of anglers and non-anglers with his two television series *Go Fishing.* He is currently working on a third series.

CHRIS YATES enjoys all aspects of the sport from gudgeon fishing in a punt to salmon spinning on the Wye, but is best known as a carp fisherman. He has been thinking about carp, he says, from the age of five when he was shown a large specimen by an old angler. His individual stalking approach to carp fishing has resulted in a personal best catch to 51½ lb. A contributor to various angling magazines, he is author of the highly acclaimed *Casting at the Sun* (1986).

The publishers are grateful for permission to reproduce illustrations on the following pages:

John Bailey 4 7 8 9 14

Trevor Housby 40 41 42 43 47

Mike Millman 95 96 97 98 99 100 101 102 103 104 105 106 107

Ken Whitehead 18 19 20 21 22 23

John Wilson 5 6 10 11 12 13 16 17 24 84 88

Chris Yates 25 26 27